R - Prof
65.00

D1002389

Usability Testing

WITHDRAWN

R - Prof
65.00

PRACTICAL GUIDES FOR LIBRARIANS

⊚ About the Series

This innovative series written and edited for librarians by librarians provides authoritative, practical information and guidance on a wide spectrum of library processes and operations.

Books in the series are focused, describing practical and innovative solutions to a problem facing today's librarian and delivering step-by-step guidance for planning, creating, implementing, managing, and evaluating a wide range of services and programs.

The books are aimed at beginning and intermediate librarians needing basic instruction/guidance in a specific subject and at experienced librarians who need to gain knowledge in a new area or guidance in implementing a new program/service.

⊚ About the Series Editor

The **Practical Guides for Librarians** series was conceived by and is edited by M. Sandra Wood, MLS, MBA, AHIP, FMLA, Librarian Emerita, Penn State University Libraries.

M. Sandra Wood was a librarian at the George T. Harrell Library, The Milton S. Hershey Medical Center, College of Medicine, Pennsylvania State University, Hershey, PA, for over 35 years, specializing in reference, educational, and database services. Ms. Wood worked for several years as a Development Editor for Neal-Schuman Publishers.

Ms. Wood received a MLS from Indiana University and a MBA from the University of Maryland. She is a Fellow of the Medical Library Association and served as a member of MLA's Board of Directors from 1991 to 1995. Ms. Wood is founding and current editor of *Medical Reference Services Quarterly*, now in its 35th volume. She also was founding editor of the *Journal of Consumer Health on the Internet* and the *Journal of Electronic Resources in Medical Libraries* and served as editor/co-editor of both journals through 2011.

Titles in the Series

1. *How to Teach: A Practical Guide for Librarians* by Beverley E. Crane
2. *Implementing an Inclusive Staffing Model for Today's Reference Services* by Julia K. Nims, Paula Storm, and Robert Stevens
3. *Managing Digital Audiovisual Resources: A Practical Guide for Librarians* by Matthew C. Mariner
4. *Outsourcing Technology: A Practical Guide for Librarians* by Robin Hastings
5. *Making the Library Accessible for All: A Practical Guide for Librarians* by Jane Vincent
6. *Discovering and Using Historical Geographical Resources on the Web: A Practical Guide for Librarians* by Eva H. Dodsworth and L. W. Laliberté
7. *Digitization and Digital Archiving: A Practical Guide for Librarians* by Elizabeth R. Leggett
8. *Makerspaces: A Practical Guide for Librarians* by John J. Burke
9. *Implementing Web-Scale Discovery Services: A Practical Guide for Librarians* by JoLinda Thompson
10. *Using iPhones and iPads: A Practical Guide for Librarians* by Matthew Connolly and Tony Cosgrave
11. *Usability Testing: A Practical Guide for Librarians* by Rebecca Blakiston

Usability Testing
A Practical Guide
for Librarians

Rebecca Blakiston

PRACTICAL GUIDES FOR LIBRARIANS, NO. 11

CALDWELL COUNTY PUBLIC LIBRARY
120 Hospital Avenue
Lenoir, North Carolina 28645

ROWMAN & LITTLEFIELD
Lanham • Boulder • New York • London

Published by Rowman & Littlefield
A wholly owned subsidiary of The Rowman & Littlefield Publishing Group, Inc.
4501 Forbes Boulevard, Suite 200, Lanham, Maryland 20706
www.rowman.com

16 Carlisle Street, London W1D 3BT, United Kingdom

Copyright © 2015 by Rowman & Littlefield

All rights reserved. No part of this book may be reproduced in any form or by any electronic
or mechanical means, including information storage and retrieval systems, without written
permission from the publisher, except by a reviewer who may quote passages in a review.

British Library Cataloguing in Publication Information Available

Library of Congress Cataloging-in-Publication Data

Blakiston, Rebecca, 1983–
    Usability testing : a practical guide for librarians / Rebecca Blakiston.
       pages cm
    Includes bibliographical references and index.
    ISBN 978-1-4422-2899-3 (pbk. : alk. paper) — ISBN 978-1-4422-2900-6 (ebook : alk.
    paper) 1. Library Web sites—Design. 2. Library Web sites—Testing. 3. User-centered
    system design. 4. Web site development. I. Title.
    Z674.75.W67B58 2015
    006.701'9—dc23   2014024454

♾™ The paper used in this publication meets the minimum requirements of American
National Standard for Information Sciences—Permanence of Paper for Printed Library
Materials, ANSI/NISO Z39.48-1992.

Printed in the United States of America

Contents

List of Tables and Figures

 Tables

⑥ Figures

Preface

In our daily lives, we interact with a variety of websites, tools, products, and services in order to both complete tasks and find answers to our questions. The best experiences are usually effortless. The worst experiences are those that seem to take additional work or be complicated, or perhaps just seem broken altogether. How often do you get frustrated when trying to complete what should be a simple task? Perhaps you are trying to sign into your account on a website, download an app to your phone, or set your signature line within your e-mail. Or maybe your experience crosses into the physical environment—you are trying to buy produce at a self-checkout machine in a grocery store, or locate a building in a large complex using a printed map. How exasperated do you get when you encounter challenges in trying to get things done or find what you are looking for?

Let's not cause these types of frustrations for library users. In *Usability Testing: A Practical Guide for Librarians*, you will learn how to discover usability problems with your library website by observing people actually trying to use it. Then perhaps most importantly, you will learn how to go about fixing those problems.

I've known that usability is important for quite some time. In fact, I was assigned to read Steve Krug's best seller, *Don't Make Me Think! A Common Sense Approach to Web Usability*, in my library graduate program. Good user experience (UX) design actually has some close connections to librarianship: it relates to information-seeking behavior, information architecture, and discovery and findability of information.

In 2008, I was hired as a reference and instruction librarian. Surprisingly, I found myself encountering the issue of usability—and lack of usability—pretty directly on a daily basis. When you are helping people with their research, you quickly notice the usability of library websites, discovery tools, and databases. Even if you aren't thinking about frustrations as "usability problems," you are likely noticing what is working well and what isn't. You learn which tools you prefer to use because they are intuitive to use, have more useful features, and/or get you to the content you need more seamlessly. In my work providing research assistance, I often found myself advocating to improve the usefulness of the website and associated research databases.

My focus on improving the user experience didn't go unnoticed, and in 2010, I was assigned as our library's first website product manager. With new title in hand, I was able to spearhead our UX efforts. But how? I had some very minimal knowledge of usability testing and knew that it was important, but had never thought to do it myself. The only experience our library had with usability testing in recent memory was a couple years earlier when an outside company conducted usability testing for us. They let us participate by watching from an observation room, and demonstrated why it was important, but it seemed like something that should really be left to the experts.

I spent the first few months as website product manager soaking up knowledge. I read Steve Krug's follow-up book, *Rocket Surgery Made Easy: A Do-It-Yourself Guide to Finding and Fixing Usability Problems*. I attended Usability Week, a training camp of sorts organized by the Nielsen Norman Group, which included a day-long workshop on "Guerilla Usability Testing." With new knowledge in hand, I realized, "Hey, maybe this is something I can do! It's not that hard, and *any* usability testing is better than *no* usability testing."

So before I knew it, I gathered some candy bars and was out there in our library lobby conducting on-the-fly intercept usability testing with students who happened to be passing by. I was walking with our web developer to the student union to conduct usability testing. Then I was training student workers to do informal testing several times a month. In 2012, I began teaching a four-week course for librarians on the topic of do-it-yourself usability testing through Library Juice Academy.

Let's be honest. There are lots of books about usability testing. Steve Krug's *Rocket Surgery Made Easy* is fantastic. *The Handbook of Usability Testing* is also a great text and gets into some of the detail that a practical guide such as this couldn't handle. But libraries are unique in many ways, and *Usability Testing: A Practical Guide for Librarians* is geared toward the specific needs of libraries. We have challenges of budgets and staffing, yet often have prime locations in the heart of communities in which we serve. We also have complex search functionality and often act as a portal to other resources that we have minimal if any control over.

The purpose of *Usability Testing: A Practical Guide for Librarians* is to walk you through the steps to do this at your own library, even with a minimal budget and small staffing. It is geared toward people with no knowledge or experience with usability testing, but also contains information for the more savvy UXers who are looking for practical advice and new inspiration on how to approach their work.

I recommend reading the book in sequence, since chapters build upon each other, but it is also possible to read just the sections most relevant to you at the moment. The book is essentially organized into three general sections.

The first two chapters are background and introductory in nature. In the first chapter, you'll learn why usability testing matters and how to make a case for it at your library. In chapter 2, we'll talk about the fundamentals, and why it is possible for any library, of any size, to conduct its own usability testing.

The middle section, and the bulk of the book, is the practical, how-to-actually-do-it content. In chapter 3, you'll identify who your users are and what they are trying to do on your website. Next, you'll explore the many options available to you for testing, as chapter 4 covers methods that require varying levels of resources. In chapter 5, you will plan for the day of testing by figuring out who, what, where, when, and how. With all planning completed, in chapter 6, we will walk through the actual usability test, including the introductory script, facilitation tips, and fundamentals of good note taking. To end this section, we get to perhaps the most challenging part in chapter 7: making sense of the results and acting upon them.

With methods and techniques in hand, the final two chapters move on to the practical application of these methods at your library. In chapter 8, you will explore methods for building ongoing usability testing into your work. Finally, in chapter 9, you will get advice on how to keep up the momentum over the long term.

My intention is for this book to be as practical as possible, so it is filled with examples and answers to common questions. I hope that it gives you the inspiration and tools to do meaningful usability testing no matter your available resources. I also hope it encourages you to conduct usability testing at all stages of your web projects and advocate for the user experience with everything you do.

Acknowledgments

Thanks to all my dear friends, family, and colleagues who made this book possible. Of course, a huge appreciation goes to Sandy Wood, who has been a responsive, supportive editor who has helped me through every step of the way. Recognition also goes to all my graduate assistants and student workers who have conducted usability testing and provided many of the examples used in this book: Rachel Hawes, Monique Perez, Odell Howell, M'Balia Thomas, Christy Bear, Samantha Barry, and Nevin Kohler. Special thanks to Rachel, who also reviewed some chapters and gave me valuable feedback, and to Jenny Gubernick and Angie Brown, who volunteered their time to contribute to our web projects and helped remind me that we do really interesting and important work.

A huge thanks has to go to the whole website crew who inspire me daily: Ginger Bidwell, Andrew See, Gabriel Luethje, Shoshana Mayden, Mike Hagedon, and Jeff Turman. It is because of all of you that I continue to love my job and enjoy coming to work every day.

Thanks also goes out to Michael Brewer and Jeremy Frumkin, who, as unofficial sponsors of the website road map, have helped me get administrative support to move forward a number of user-centered web initiatives. Also, a shout out to the entire Instructional Services Team, who have been truly supportive and flexible throughout the book-writing process. I enjoy working with each and every one of you. A special thanks to Yvonne Mery, who is a kindred spirit and happened to be writing a book at the same time, for lending an ear and giving me much-appreciated advice throughout the process. And a special thanks to Cheryl Cuillier for helping me think through sentences and providing her fabulous editor's eye, not to mention being the best officemate a person could ask for.

Thank you to Trevor Smith, who first introduced me to *Don't Make Me Think*, and Steve Krug, who wrote it and is a super nice guy to boot. And to Heather O'Neill for encouraging me and proving again that UXers are the kindest people you'll meet. Thanks to Rory Litwin, who unknowingly set the ball rolling by inviting me to teach a class for Library Juice Academy. And appreciation goes to the other instructors who helped put together the user experience certificate program: Nicole Capdarest-Arest, Carolyn Ellis, Sonali Mishra, and Susan Teague Rector.

Thanks to my parents for teaching me I can do anything I set my mind to, and my brother and sister for being siblings you actually enjoy spending time with. And thanks to Scott, for putting up with my many days of sitting at the computer endlessly drinking coffee and ignoring him and the puppies. His love and support keeps me grounded and brings me life's greatest joy.

CHAPTER 1

Why Usability Testing Matters

IN THIS CHAPTER

Find out

▷ Why the usability of your website impacts your library's success

▷ Why usability testing is a great way to gather authentic data about your website and user behavior

▷ Why user research in general is important to discovering your usability problems

▷ Why it's important to pay attention to the overall user experience beyond your website

▷ Why usability testing results can guide significant improvements to the user experience

---

IT IS ESSENTIAL FOR LIBRARY WEBSITES to be both usable and enjoyable in order for libraries to stay relevant into the future. In this chapter, you will find out why your website and the user experience matter to the success of your organization. You will also learn why usability testing is an authentic and effective way to test your website's design, navigation, and content, and why the results of testing can help you make significant improvements to the user experience.

Your Website Matters

An organization's website is often the primary access point for users to find out about the services, resources, and information it provides. Library organizations are no different. With many information resources now completely digital, and many library services being provided virtually, a growing number of people visit the library entirely online. College students can conduct library research for their assignments, request electronic materials through interlibrary loan, and get research help from librarians for four years without ever entering the physical building. Community members can download popular e-books, research information on grants, and donate money to their public libraries without even knowing the location of their local branch. On top of this, there are a growing number of virtual libraries and digital repositories that have no physical public spaces whatsoever.

Your website matters because it is a primary access point. Regardless of the size, location, or type of library, a library's website and web presence continue to grow in importance as users expect to access what they need, when they need it, and where they need it, which is often from a distance. The library website is now one of the primary mechanisms by which librarians connect users with all of the things their libraries have to offer.

Your website is a virtual representation of your organization. The experience users have on your website can determine whether they sign up for a library card, use a particular service, access a particular resource, donate money, fund a grant, or recommend your library to family, friends, peers, and colleagues. The experience users have will determine whether they stay on your website or give up and seek out an alternative. If a user has an unpleasant experience, even just once, that user might never return.

User expectations continue to rise as the web becomes an increasingly essential part of daily life. Start to pay close attention to interactions you have online, and you may notice that your own expectations are quite high. Most information you digest is electronic, and you expect websites you visit to be useful, credible, and easy to use. You expect to find answers to your questions quickly, and to be able to complete tasks seamlessly. There are websites that you enjoy visiting, and there are websites that are frustrating and that you dread having to use. You may find that you have to use frustrating websites for one reason or another, perhaps because it is required for work or school, but the reality is that if you had the choice and didn't have to use a frustrating website, you wouldn't.

The vast majority of organizations have websites, and it is important to have a website in order to stay credible and visible. Yet an organization with an outdated, unattractive, or unusable website also loses a substantial amount of credibility. Users will only access these types of websites if they *have* to and there is no alternative. Let's work to make library websites ones that users enjoy, and that they use not just because they *have* to, but because they *want* to.

A good, usable website will instill trust and loyalty in your users. You will receive more positive feedback, online reviews, and satisfaction ratings. You will experience more return visitors and more use of the services and resources you provide through your website. Because of this, you may get more funding, including more donations, more grants, and more support from your community. For this reason, it is important to invest the staff and financial resources into making your website as useful and enjoyable as possible.

With complex content, multifaceted organizational structures, broad distribution of website-related responsibilities, and reliance on outside vendors, libraries often struggle in designing and maintaining websites that are easy to use. But librarians must overcome these obstacles and find effective, sustainable ways to assess and improve library websites. You must be better than the alternative. This is vital if you are to say relevant and useful to the communities that you serve.

Usability testing is a tried-and-true method for gathering feedback from users. Usability testing first came into practice long before the days of web design for testing various types of products, but it has been particularly popular for testing how users interact with websites. Usability testing is a research method that tests websites in a realistic fashion to see how well they are (or are not) meeting the needs and expectations of users.

In planning for usability testing, you first define tasks that a user might want to accomplish on your website, whether it is finding the answer to a question, using a service, or accessing a resource. During the usability test, a facilitator reads one or more scenarios out loud to a participant who is an actual or potential user of your website. The facilitator and a note taker then observe the participant using the website and trying to complete the given task. Generally, the same test will be conducted multiple times with different participants. As they are attempting to complete the task, participants are usually encouraged to speak out loud as much as possible, expressing their thoughts and emotions along the way, as well as verbalizing their decision-making processes. The facilitator assists by keeping participants talking, keeping them calm, and asking any probing questions as appropriate. However, the facilitator must be careful to not interfere with the participants' interactions with the website. In order to discover results that are as authentic as possible, as if the participants were attempting to complete the tasks independently, it is important for the facilitator to not lead them in any particular direction.

By observing the behavior of a user in this realistic context and by listening to how the participant describes his or her experience, you will gain valuable insight. You will learn how users think about your content: the mental models they have, the words they use to describe things, and what they understand or don't understand. You will learn how they attempt to navigate through your content: what trigger words they look for, what menu items and labels they select, and what links they choose to click on. Perhaps most importantly, you will learn where they struggle: what content they can't find or don't understand, at what point they get lost or have to navigate back, and when they fail to complete a task.

You will most likely discover usability problems that you didn't know existed and usability problems in unexpected places. Many times, you will discover problems not

A SOMEWHAT ARTIFICIAL ENVIRONMENT
CAN STILL PRODUCE AUTHENTIC RESULTS

While the intention is to discover what users would actually do in a real situation, there is certainly a level of artificiality to usability testing. Participants are given scenarios they may or may not be able to relate to, being observed by people who wouldn't normally be observing them, and using technology and location they might not normally use. That said, researchers have found time and time again that usability testing uncovers realistic findings. World-renowned user experience researcher Jakob Nielsen (2005) explained that the power of engagement and the suspension of disbelief are the two main factors that cause participants to behave as they would out in the real world.

associated with the particular task but that are still problems that ought to be addressed. The problems you discover are actual, authentic problems that your website visitors experience. The good news is that once the problems are identified, you then will be able to tackle those problems and implement solutions.

Usability testing is the key method for getting feedback on the overall user experience within the context of how easy (or hard) it is to complete actual tasks. This method allows you to gather data about all elements of your website, including the visual design, information architecture, navigation elements, and content itself.

Many other user research methods exist and are useful for a variety of purposes. To embrace user experience design and to have a truly user-centered website, you should incorporate a variety of user research methods into your design, development, and content creation workflows. Talk to and gather input from users often, and utilize a variety of methods, including focus groups, interviews, card sorting, and multivariate testing. Usability testing is just one particular user research method to have within your toolbox, but it is perhaps the most important and authentic of the lot. Usability testing remains the primary choice of designers, developers, and user experience advocates because of its authenticity and inherent usefulness as you watch actual people using your website.

Keep in mind that the type of usability testing described in this book is small-scale, unscientific, do-it-yourself testing that is realistic for a library to manage completely in house. This differs from larger scale, more controlled usability testing that is often conducted by usability professionals. While ideally you could have usability professionals organize all of your usability testing, you likely do not have usability professionals on staff who dedicate their lives' work to this type of effort. It is quite possible that usability testing doesn't even fall within any particular person's job description at your institution. So you need to work within the limitations of what is available to you. The type of usability testing being described here, while less scientific than that organized by usability professionals, still leads to authentic results that are of tremendous value. Additionally, it is both practical and sustainable for any type of library.

The User Experience Matters

The importance of investigating how users interact with the offerings you provide is not just limited to the context of your website. We live in a multichannel world, and usability testing is a useful undertaking to consider across channels and with every service or product that you provide. When thinking about the primary tasks of your users, you may discover a myriad of contexts that takes them beyond the interface of the library website.

The tasks your users want to complete will likely involve systems or web products associated with your website but potentially beyond the scope of what your web team generally focuses on. These systems may live outside your website, be less controlled, and be managed or overseen by a variety of departments. Such systems include your integrated library system (including your library catalog), web-based discovery tool(s), subscription databases, and interlibrary loan systems. Users may be interacting with an assortment of other features such as instructional tutorials, knowledge management systems, room reservation applications, and live chat functionality. While a library may separate these systems internally within the organizational structure, users likely don't distinguish these systems as they are trying to use your website to find what they need or to complete a task.

You may also provide web-based experiences beyond the traditional web context. For instance, you may provide native mobile apps for library services or other functions. You likely also provide virtual communication mechanisms, such as e-mails and text messages. Perhaps you also promote services and communicate generally with your users using social media. Again, these pieces of the user experience might be managed by distinct departments within your organization, but they all contribute to the user experience and are deserving of usability testing.

In addition, many library users do not start on the library website. You ought to pay attention to other access points to your resources and services, ones that are somewhat beyond your control, because they play an important role in the overall user experience. For instance, if researchers use Google, how do they gain access to your digitized archives? If researchers use Google Scholar, how do they gain access to your subscription content? If students use your college website to search, how will they find information about software installed in your computer labs or laptops you have available for checkout? These are all pieces within the user journey, and so they cannot be ignored.

This concept can be taken even further as you look beyond the virtual space. User experience also includes services that exist in the physical space and services that exist across both arenas. In fact, many library services will certainly fall in this last category and include both web-based and physical aspects. For instance, you might have a retrieval process for getting materials off the shelves for your users. This process begins on your website, at which point a user makes a request through your discovery or catalog system; next, an e-mail or text message is sent to the user; and finally the user enters the physical library building, navigates using library signage to look for the hold shelf, retrieves the item based on whatever organization system you are using, and checks it out, perhaps using a self-checkout machine. This is an entire user journey, and to test the usability of a particular service, you may need to test all components within that journey: the online request process, the e-mail notification, the library signage, the hold shelf itself, and the checkout machine. In other words, even if you have a usable website, it doesn't mean you have a usable experience overall.

Given this, try to keep in mind that the same techniques described in this book for testing the usability of a website can be used for testing the usability of a myriad of other virtual and physical services and products. Consider the usability of everything from your physical signage in the building to your self-checkout machines to your interlibrary loan process. For simplicity's sake, I will be referring to testing "websites," but feel free to substitute this for your own context to X service, Y product, or Z process.

⑥ Usability Testing Results Matter

By observing how users interact with the features of your website, you learn where they succeed and where they struggle. This insight is absolutely essential to knowing where improvements need to be made and where to focus your design, development, and content efforts.

In a typical usability test, you will discover a number of usability problems that you didn't know existed. Oftentimes, within minutes of a usability test, you will learn about a single element on your website that is difficult to use or to understand. Fortunately, there is often a simple change that will make a vast improvement, and that change can be implemented quickly. After a few rounds of testing and tweaking your website, you will have made great strides toward a more usable and enjoyable user experience.

You may also discover larger, more complicated problems that will take more thought and more testing to fix. The good news is that whatever problems are discovered, you will be able to recognize them and make efforts toward fixing them. Later in this book, you will learn in more detail how to interpret results, brainstorm solutions, and go about implementing them.

Usability testing is most effective when conducted in an ongoing, systematic way. The services and resources that libraries provide are constantly evolving, which means that changes to your website are inevitable. User behavior and expectations are also changing at a rapid pace. Web technology and options for content management, web development, and design continue to expand, as does the myriad of devices used for accessing the web.

In order to stay relevant and useful to users, libraries should establish sustainable, on-going methods for conducting usability testing. The results of usability testing, especially when conducted systematically, can guide decision making for all aspects of your website and can immensely improve the overall user experience.

Key Points

In-house usability testing is not only feasible, but it is practical, sustainable, and has the potential to lead to remarkable improvements of the content, design, and layout of your website. Remember:

- Your website is a primary access point to your library's resources and services.
- Usability testing puts your users in a realistic context and gives you authentic results.
- Your website is only one piece of the user experience; a user-centered approach should be used in contexts beyond your website.
- Results of usability testing can guide your decisions and allow you to take great leaps toward a better user experience.

So now that you're convinced, let's talk about the elements required to actually go about doing it.

Reference

Nielsen, Jakob. 2005. "Authentic Behavior in User Testing." Nielsen Norman Group, February 14. http://www.nngroup.com/articles/authentic-behavior-in-user-testing/.

CHAPTER 2

Conducting Your Own Usability Testing

IN THIS CHAPTER

Find out

▷ What basic knowledge and skills sets you will need

▷ What financial and staffing resources you will need

▷ How much time you will need

AT ITS CORE, USABILITY TESTING is really not that complicated. It is a simple and practical user research method, and it's something that any librarian, in any setting, with any background has the capability of doing. Web usability is a growing area of study. You will not become a usability professional by reading this book, but you will learn enough to conduct useful usability tests. In this chapter, you will gain an understanding of the basic knowledge and skill sets required: familiarity with user behavior, good facilitation techniques, and problem-solving skills. You will also learn what financial and staffing resources are necessary and how much time you will need to dedicate to testing.

Usability Testing Is Not Hard

Learning how to conduct a usability test is not as difficult as you might think. The key things you need to know are covered within this book and do not require any previous knowledge or experience with user research methods. They simply require some dedicated time and a keen interest in improving the user experience.

Understanding User Behavior

The first key component to usability testing is the process of establishing your users' primary tasks. To do this successfully, you need to have a basic, fundamental understanding of your audience and user behavior, and you need to be an advocate for the user.

As a librarian, you might already have frequent interactions with your users. Perhaps you work in public services and regularly staff a service desk where you personally meet with large numbers of users, answering their questions and providing them with information. Perhaps you work in reference or research services and schedule appointments to sit down one-on-one with users and assist them with in-depth research questions. Maybe you assist users through other communication channels, such as phone, e-mail, chat, text messaging, or social media. If you work in an education setting, you might be involved with instruction and meet both individually with instructors about their coursework as well as with classes full of students. Regardless of your position within the library, you likely have some level of interaction with users.

These types of interactions can be a huge advantage to understanding user behavior. You get to know your users on a personal level. So as you have these interactions, pay attention to the common questions users have, the language and terms that they use to describe things, and their general mind-set when they approach a problem.

If you aren't in a position where you regularly interact with users, you may consider finding a way to make this happen. There are a variety of ways to approach this, and none of them are difficult or time-consuming. At minimum, you could meet regularly with library staff members that do have these sorts of interactions. For instance, you could meet monthly with representatives from reference, instruction, and public services, listening to their ideas and soliciting feedback on upcoming website changes. Additionally, you could include a user-centered public services staff member on your web team, involving that voice in all discussions related to the website. If you are unable to work regular hours at a service desk, you could occasionally schedule a few hours to observe interactions at the desk. Similarly, you could regularly volunteer to respond to some questions or ask to see transcripts from chat or e-mail interactions.

In chapter 3, you will learn more about how to define your audience and their tasks, regardless of your current role within the library. Fortunately, for most librarians, your users are not difficult to find and are interacting with library staff members every day. Pay attention to their behavior and always keep them in mind. To be successful at conducting usability testing, you must become an advocate for the user.

Writing Good Scenarios

Once your tasks are established for testing, you will need to translate them into scenarios that are realistic, are easy to understand, and do not lead the participant in any particular direction. This technique is helpful when conducting any sort of user research. You may have written surveys or test questions in the past. As you were writing those questions, you had to be sure they were understandable and that you were not leading the participant toward (or away from) any particular answer or down any particular path. This is the same concept as you write scenarios for usability testing. Writing non-leading scenarios can take some practice, but it isn't difficult and it is a similar skill required for many different types of research studies.

Even if your scenarios turn out to be leading or confusing to participants, you can fix them. You will likely recognize that this is the case during an initial test, and you can then amend the scenario for the next test. Since this is less scientific usability testing, it is OK to be flexible and adjust your scenarios as needed.

Being a Good Facilitator

During the test itself, you will likely play the role called facilitator or moderator. The term *facilitator* implies a slightly more active role than *moderator* and will be used throughout this book.

Becoming a good facilitator is mostly a matter of learning techniques of the trade and then getting a chance to practice them. One thing that can be a challenge initially is keeping calm and objective. If you are even partially responsible for the website you are testing, which is often the case, you may have a hard time when you find out that things don't work as intended. You may take offense or become upset if participants do not click where you expected them to click. As facilitator, you must remain objective and you cannot give participants advice or suggestions. It can be difficult to do this, though, as you may have to watch participants fail a task, and you will be unable to help or "correct" their behavior. This can be particularly hard for those who work in public services and have a customer service mentality, as you are used to helping users as part of your day-to-day work.

Keeping calm and optimistic, and avoiding getting frustrated, is an important skill for any facilitator to master. Remember that it is normal to discover usability problems, that nobody's website is perfect, and that all information you gather is useful information. Even if you aren't the perfect facilitator at first, you will still find out something useful. Facilitation will get easier and you will become better at it over time.

Another skill a facilitator must have is the ability to know when to ask questions and when to keep quiet. You need to keep the participant talking, but you need to avoid distracting him or her unnecessarily. Additionally, you need to know when to end a particular task and move on, and when to end the session itself. Again, it may not go perfectly the first time, but these are all learnable skills that just take practice and patience.

Making Sense of Your Results

Analyzing results from testing can be a challenge, but the ability to talk through the user's behavior and brainstorm possible solutions is no more difficult than tackling a design problem you discover outside of conducting any usability testing. You likely have some experience doing this already as you discover usability problems through other mechanisms, such as general feedback from users or staff members. Having a web team or dedicated usability team is a big advantage as you tackle usability problems, as you can brainstorm possible solutions, bounce ideas off each other, and share any user experience expertise that might be in the room. As you conduct more usability testing, you will naturally become better at fixing usability problems. It is also important to spend time keeping up-to-date on results of the latest research studies published through professional user experience organizations. Growing knowledge internally will be of great benefit to addressing usability problems quickly and effectively when they are discovered.

Coming up with feasible solutions isn't always easy and you might not always come up with the best solution on the first try, but testing again and tweaking again will undoubtedly lead to improvements. It is extremely rare to discover a usability problem and come up with a solution that makes it *worse*, and even making it just a little bit better can have big impact on your users.

⌾ Usability Testing Doesn't Need to Be Expensive

Incentives

Librarians may be hesitant to conduct usability testing, at least in an ongoing way, due to lack of both financial and staff resources. The primary cost associated with usability testing is incentives to encourage users to participate. Costs for incentives can be substantial. For one-hour usability sessions, you may offer gift cards of $25 or more to each participant. Even just five tests per month will add up to a budget of $1,500–$3,000 annually for these types of tests. This may be a reasonable investment to improve your website, but it may be impractical for many libraries dealing with tough budgetary times. Fortunately, there is a more cost-effective approach.

Incentives can be cheap, if not free, to the organization. When determining what level of incentive is most appropriate for your situation, think about the approximate amount of time you are asking each participant to sit with you. For example, a full hour test will require a greater incentive than a 15-minute test. So while traditional usability testing is scheduled in one-hour blocks, this doesn't have to be the case. Depending upon the task(s) you are asking the participant to complete, you can conduct a test in a shorter amount of time. So if you would give a participant a $25 gift card for an hour session, perhaps you could give them $10 gift card for a half-hour session. Further, you can avoid purchasing gift cards all together by exploring alternate incentives such as T-shirts, water bottles, snacks, or tickets to enter a raffle for a larger prize.

Another aspect to consider in your planning is the particular audience that you want to participate. What is your audience's availability, and do you have a sense of their willingness to volunteer for a research study? This can contribute to both the cost of incentives as well as whether you need to schedule usability sessions in advance or if you can conduct them on the fly. For instance, students available in the college library might be more willing to sit with you for a free tote bag and a bottle of water than a potential donor or a faculty member would, especially if the donor or faculty member has to be contacted individually to set up an appointment in advance.

When determining what incentives are best, consider your audience's availability and how easy or hard it is to find volunteers to participate. Also consider the length of the usability test and what might motivate people to take time out of their day. Feel free to get creative and if you are on a tight budget, think about things your library already has on hand or things that are completely free to the library. The examples in table 2.1 might give you some ideas.

Technology

Another potential cost associated with testing is hardware and software. Obviously, you will need some sort of computer for conducting the test. This computer could be a desktop, laptop, tablet, or even a smartphone or other handheld device. Hopefully, you have something at your disposal already, but it might be something that requires a purchase. This is

Table 2.1. Incentive Examples

EXAMPLE PARTICIPANT	LENGTH OF USABILITY TEST	POSSIBLE INCENTIVES
Student	10 minutes	King-sized candy bar Piece of fresh fruit Bag of chips or trail mix "Study Tips" magnet "I Read Banned Books" button
Student	30 minutes	Raffle ticket for an iPad Raffle ticket for their own study table in the library "Keep Calm, Study On" T-shirt "I Read Banned Books" tote bag $5 gift card to the campus book store
Member of the public	30 minutes	Raffle ticket for a Kindle $10 gift card to Friends of the Library book store Coffee mug with vendor logo
Faculty member	1 hour	$25 gift card to a campus coffee shop "I Support Open Access" tote bag Polo shirt with university logo

particularly true if you are trying to test out different types of devices to ensure your website is usable on different screen sizes, different operating systems, and on touch screens.

Also, usability tests traditionally tend to involve recording the session live and streaming it to a room for stakeholders to observe. Software designed specifically for usability testing, such as Morae and Silverback, will usually capture and record the computer screen, including highlighting the cursor and mouse clicks. It will also record the audio and video of users as they participate in the usability study, so you can capture their facial expressions and narration. The software often has additional functionality, allowing you to indicate when you move to a different task for easier playback after the fact, and allowing you to work with the recording later by marking key moments, adding comments, and highlighting activity on the screen. The software may even have stakeholders from remote locations make live comments during the session using a chat box.

Streaming live, recording, and reviewing a usability session can be helpful for communicating with stakeholders as well as analyzing the results among your web team. While software specifically created for usability testing is the best option, there are cheaper or more readily available alternatives, as well. If you create library tutorials, you may already have screen-capturing software, such as Captivate, Camtasia, or Screenium. These tools, while designed for creating online learning objects, can also be used to capture and record usability tests. There are also several free, simpler screen-capturing tools that can be used to make a basic recording of the screen, including mouse movements. Table 2.2 lists some screen-capturing software including some features and cost.

In addition to the recording software, you will need an audio recording device. This could be a microphone that is built into the computer you are using, or built into a webcam, or it could be a stand-alone microphone or headset. Even if you don't have access to any of the recording tools, you can use a webcam with a built-in microphone, use a camcorder, or simply don't record it. If you take concise notes, you don't necessarily need a recording to refer to later or share with stakeholders.

Table 2.2. Software and Hardware Examples

SOFTWARE	CAPTURES ON-SCREEN ACTIVITY	CAPTURES PARTICIPANTS' FACIAL EXPRESSIONS	PROVIDES LIVE OBSERVATION	ALLOWS YOU TO MARK/COMMENT ON RECORDING	COST
Morae	x	x	x	x	$1,995.00
Silverback	x	x		x	$69.95
Camtasia	x			x	$299.00
Captivate	x			x	$899.00
Jing	x				Free
Screenium	x	x		x	$39.99
Screenr	x				Free
Webcam		x			Varies

Consider what resources are available to you and what level of communication with stakeholders and your web team is necessary. You can then select the software and hardware that is most appropriate to your situation.

Staffing

Lack of staff resources can also be a deterrent. Usability testing, though, does not have to be time intensive and is usually conducted by just two people: the facilitator and the note taker. So, usability testing can be conducted even if you are in a smaller library with just a few staff members. It can even work if you are literally the only available person to conduct the usability testing. It is possible to do testing completely by yourself, acting as both facilitator and note taker. So you can plan, conduct, and analyze results of a usability test even within a single-person library.

The role of facilitator or note taker can be played by librarians or staff members, but you can also train interns, student workers, or even volunteers to conduct testing for you. As you will learn, it is not hard, and so high-paid staff members do not necessarily need to be involved in order for it to be successful.

ⓖ Usability Testing Doesn't Need to Be Time-Consuming

Some time commitment is necessary, but it's not as much as you might think. You can conduct usability testing in an ongoing way without dedicating substantial amounts of time to it. Usability testing in small doses is still useful, and keep in mind that even a small amount of testing can return enormous value.

Establishing an ongoing schedule is helpful. Steve Krug (2010) recommends a "once-a-month" model in which you dedicate just one morning, about five hours, each month to conducting usability testing and discussing the results. A variation on this model, perhaps once every two months or three times a semester, might work best for your particular situation. The idea is that short but frequent tests are the most effective.

You can also establish a process to determine when conducting usability testing is most beneficial and dedicate more time to it at particular moments. It is usually best to test early on in a project, for instance, rather than to wait until a project is nearly completed. You may conduct significant testing during a redesign or rebuild project, then lessen the time dedicated to testing in the following year. For a website that already exists, you may want to conduct testing on particular types of changes. For instance, certain substantial or impactful website changes might benefit more from a usability test over smaller changes. In chapter 8, you will read more about methods for practical, sustainable models for ongoing usability testing.

Additionally, the time scheduled per usability testing session can be flexible. Sessions are often scheduled for a full hour. This means you could conduct four sessions in a single morning. But you could manage the tests differently and have them last 30, 15, or even 5 minutes, depending on your goals and what sort of tasks you are testing. Keep in mind that many of our web interactions are mere minutes if not seconds long. Many tasks can be completed in moments.

Further, you don't actually need to test that many people. A Nielsen Norman Group study found that testing just five people will allow you to discover the majority of the usability problems, and that it is actually not worth the return on investment to test more than five people (Nielsen 2012). So if one usability test lasts just 15 minutes, you could complete a round of testing in just over an hour and discover most of your usability problems related to a particular task.

To sum up, the time set aside for testing need not be substantial to be effective; it just needs to be ongoing commitment.

Key Points

Usability testing is something that is within reach, no matter what your situation, and doing usability testing in some manner is most certainly better than not doing it at all. Remember:

- You probably already know quite a bit about your users, and if you don't, you can learn about your users pretty easily.
- Writing understandable and non-leading scenarios is a good skill to have in general, and you can always adjust them if you need to.
- Being a good facilitator takes some practice, but you will get there.
- Analyzing results and developing solutions is probably something you do already, and you will get better at it over time.
- Usability testing can be done on the cheap.
- You don't need many staff resources.
- You don't need much time.

Even if you don't master the knowledge and skills necessary for the perfect usability test, it is still worthwhile. Remember that it is OK if you don't know everything yet, and it's OK if things don't go perfectly the first time. You will learn a little along the way and improve your skills over time. You probably won't make anything worse than it is, and more likely you will make significant improvements.

Let's move on to how you will actually go about conducting usability testing. The first step is to find out who your audience is and what they are trying to do.

References

Krug, Steve. 2010. *Rocket Surgery Made Easy: The Do-It-Yourself Guide to Finding and Fixing Usability Problems*. Berkeley, CA: New Riders.

Nielsen, Jakob. 2012. "How Many Test Users in a Usability Study?" Nielsen Norman Group. June 4. http://www.nngroup.com/articles/how-many-test-users/.

CHAPTER 3

Identifying Your Audience and Its Tasks

IN THIS CHAPTER

Find out

▷ Why knowing your audience will help you conduct more useful usability tests

▷ How you can use various methods to learn about your audience needs and behaviors

▷ How to define your primary audience

▷ How to establish primary tasks for your primary audience segments

▷ Why creating personas that represent your primary audience is beneficial

UNDERSTANDING WHO IS USING YOUR WEBSITE and what they are trying to do is an important step in planning for usability testing. It will help you recruit suitable participants, define appropriate tasks, and prioritize which tasks should be tested. In this chapter, you will explore various ways in which you can gather data about your users. You will learn how to use this data to define your primary audience as well as their primary tasks related to your website. With all this information gathered, you will learn how to develop and utilize personas that represent those audiences and their tasks, further putting yourself in the mind of the user.

Knowing Your Audience Matters

Not all website users are created equal. The experience users have when accessing your website may differ depending on their background, previous experiences, technical knowledge, and subject knowledge. You also need to consider their awareness of library services, their familiarity with library terms, and their comfort level using research databases and other online searching tools. Individuals will interact with your website differently depending on all of these factors, so your usability testing results may also differ depending on who participates.

Further, you will need to determine what tasks you want to test. Libraries often have complex, multifaceted, content-rich websites. The reality is that you cannot test everything. You need to test what is most important to your users. Knowing your audience and their goals within the context of your website will help you both select and prioritize tasks for usability testing.

Keep in mind, though, that you don't usually need to recruit participants who perfectly match your primary audience demographic. You also don't need to know without a doubt the prioritized ranking of primary tasks of your audience. While these factors will give you more accurate and representative results, you will find that all usability testing—even the less controlled variety—is useful. It cannot be overstated: any usability testing is better than no usability testing.

Find Out about Your Audience

You can gather information about your audience in a variety of ways, beginning by collecting data already in existence. In all likelihood, your library collects, manages, and analyzes some type of user data in an ongoing way. It is also possible that your library has recently completed an assessment project of some kind.

Investigate what type of data is being collected already, and what particular assessment efforts may have taken place recently. This can be a starting point for defining your primary users and their website tasks. If you find that there isn't much substantive data on your audience, you may want to consider gathering more useful data in the future. Regardless of what data exists already, you will probably have to do some level of additional research to get a more accurate, full picture of your audience.

As you analyze existing data, focus on that which has been gathered within the past few years, noticing themes and trends that reflect your users' level of knowledge, experience, and skill sets. Notice what rises to the top as far as their needs related to your website, and what may influence their behavior as it relates to your website. Possible sources for data on your users include

- Environmental scanning and strategic planning
- Question logs
- Instructional data
- Class and workshop data
- Campus and community data
- Focus groups and user interviews
- Surveys and feedback forms
- Anecdotal data

Environmental Scanning and Strategic Planning

Most libraries create strategic plans to guide and prioritize their work. Strategic planning processes often involve some level of environmental scanning in which the planning group looks at data, trends, and themes within the internal and external environment. Perhaps your planning group compiles data as part of a strategic planning report. If so, this can be an excellent starting point to find out what sources of data have already been compiled and analyzed.

If your library doesn't have any formal strategic planning process, it might be worth implementing in the future. Not only will it help you understand your audience, but it will help you prioritize work related to the website. For instance, your strategic plan might highlight the growing use of handheld devices within your primary audience. Knowing this, your web team may focus on providing a better user experience from handheld devices, and may also conduct usability testing with smartphones or tablets rather than desktops or laptops.

Question Logs

Libraries with any kind of service function will have staff members who answer questions from users on a regular basis. This is an opportunity to gather a wealth of information about what questions users ask most frequently, which can then be translated into tasks on your website. This includes questions asked in person, over the phone, via chat, via text, and through e-mail. These questions will reflect the needs of your primary audience, and may include a diversity of directional and reference questions, from "What are your hours?" to "How can a find a book on this topic?"

Your library may collect this data by asking staff members to log questions they receive into an online system, such as Desk Tracker or LibAnswers. Additionally, your library might have desk observations where questions are recorded, or it might have scheduled times during the year where this type of data is collected. If nothing else, you probably have a record of e-mail interactions through your e-mail system.

One caveat when you analyze this data, though, is that a question asked in person at a service desk might not necessarily be the same type of question or as common of a question within the context of your website. For instance, "Where is your hold shelf?" might be a more common in-person question, but a less common question for website visitors. Questions asked electronically via chat, text, or e-mail might be more closely associated with tasks on the website than in-person questions.

Instructional Data

If you work in an academic library that provides teaching support for faculty and instructors, you can gather instructional statistics that can tell you which courses, which majors, and which disciplines request or receive the most library instruction. You can also find out

If you work in an academic library, ask,

- What majors or degrees tend to do the most library research?
- What classes require the most research assignments?
- What type and level of research are instructors requiring?
- What resources are most heavily used in classes?

**EXAMPLE OF USEFUL DATA
ABOUT A GENERAL EDUCATION COURSE**

A large political science course taken by nearly a third of all freshmen tends to include significant group research projects. In these courses, instructors assign the students the library's Popular vs. Scholarly tutorial and then direct students to use particular databases such as LexisNexis for newspapers and JSTOR for empirical research articles.

which students are required to conduct library research and for which classes or subject areas, and find out which particular resources are most important to these students, including which databases, research guides, or tutorials. This type of data can further inform your list of audience characteristics and website tasks.

For instance, you might find out that most first-year students have to take an English composition course. In many cases, these courses will involve a research assignment. Perhaps these courses include some level of library instruction and introduce students to research databases for the first time.

When reviewing curriculum within a particular department or major, you might find out that students within certain disciplines are an important segment of your audience. Perhaps history majors are assigned a significant number of research papers that will require complex library research, including researching primary sources. You may also find out that students within particular courses are an important audience segment. Perhaps for history majors, most research skills are taught in the foundational Introduction to the Study of History course, which tends to involve a library instruction session within your special collections. These skills are then built upon in the upper-division Capstone Research Seminar course, but these juniors and seniors rely on a research guide created collaboratively with a librarian and the instructor.

You can investigate further by looking at course research assignments to find out what type of research students are asked to conduct, including what topics, types of information, and material formats. For instance, you may discover that several large undergraduate sociology courses involve research projects that look at historical magazine advertisements, or that a popular interdisciplinary degree asks students to complete portfolios that bring together documentary films and their source materials.

As you can imagine, looking at this instructional data can begin to draw a picture of two important segments of your audience: the instructors assigning research assignments and the students completing research assignments.

Class and Workshop Data

If you work in a public library, you might organize computer classes and skills workshops. At these events, you might be collecting data on attendance, participants' previous knowledge and skill level, and their other areas of interest. This type of data may provide you with information on your users' knowledge level and background experiences, as well as their interests surrounding various topics and opportunities for continuing education.

If you work in a public library, ask,

- What classes or workshops are most popular?
- Who attends which classes or workshops (age, demographic, skill level)?
- What other data is gathered at these events?

Campus and Community Data

Most likely, some external sources are already gathering data about your audience. If you are at an academic institution, an admissions or diversity office may gather broad student and employee demographics, as well as demographics within individual schools or departments. This compiled data will likely include information on age, gender, ethnicity, and educational level or background. You may be able to find a wealth of this sort of information on your campus website. Try looking at the "About," "Admissions," and "Diversity" sections of the website, as well as looking for a recent campus strategic plan or annual report.

If you serve the broader community, you can look at census data, which will include such demographics as age, household size, ethnicity, and income. Your city may also collect local information that has more detail. The state, county, or city website ought to have this sort of information publicly available. Again, try looking online, this time at the city or county website, focusing on any "About," "Demographics," "Living," or "Diversity" sections.

You may have other audience data available to you, depending on your setting. The National Survey in Student Engagement is conducted at many higher education institutions and can provide you with data on student use of technology, experience with writing assignments, and more. Your campus might conduct other surveys of students, such as exit surveys, technology surveys, student governance surveys, and opinion surveys.

Investigate what data has already been gathered in your particular community and use it to get a bigger picture of your audience. If a piece of information is missing that is important for consideration, such as technology use or education level, you might consider conducting your own assessment to gather that data and incorporate it into your understanding of your audience.

Focus Groups and User Interviews

A great way to find out about your users' needs, as well as how your users think about things, is to ask them directly. You can invite members of your audience to attend a focus group in which they gather in a room and a facilitator asks them a series of questions. You can ask participants open-ended questions that will provide you with insight into their backgrounds, their priorities, and their behavior. Depending on your setting and goals, you can hold a broader focus group with members of varied segments of your primary audience, or you can hold a more specific focus group to delve deeper into a particular audience segment's background and behaviors.

If you are holding a focus group with diverse audience representation, such as undergraduate students and graduate students with different disciplinary interests, you might ask such general questions as

- What do you tend to use the library website for?
- How does the library help you get your classwork done?
- What library services do you use most?

A more targeted focus group could allow for more specific types of questions. Perhaps you know that English composition instructors are a significant segment of your audience, but you are struggling to define their primary website tasks. You may need to know more about their instructional processes and how they tend to use library resources in their courses. By hosting a focus group with members of this particular audience, you can gather information to help you better identify their previous knowledge and experience as well as their primary website tasks. For instance, you might ask such questions as

- How does the library help you with your teaching?
- How do you use library resources in your teaching?
- How do you go about developing your research assignments?
- Do you assign any library tutorials to your students (and if so, which ones)?
- Where do your students struggle most with their research assignments?

When planning for iterative, ongoing usability testing, you will want to focus mostly on actual primary tasks of users in the current environment. If you are creating a new website, undertaking a significant redesign, or looking to expand your website content to better serve your users, you may want to hear about services or content your website doesn't currently provide but that users desire in the future. Focus groups can be a helpful way to gather this type of information. In this example case of English composition instructors, you might ask follow-up questions such as

- Do you use the website for this? If not, what information could the website provide that would help you?
- What information could the website provide to better help your students where they struggle most?

Conducting focus groups will help you define your primary audience in more detail, identify their primary tasks, and develop some realistic scenarios that you can then use for usability testing. It will also give you insight into how you might make your website more usable in general, by understanding your users' background knowledge, needs, and behavior.

TIP FOR FOCUS GROUPS

Pay attention to the language participants use to describe things. Do they use library terms, such as *reference*, *interlibrary loan*, and *stacks*, or do they describe these things differently, perhaps as *research help*, *borrowing from other libraries*, and *bookshelves*? Understanding the terms used by actual users will help you write meaningful scenarios for usability testing as well as create more user-centered language on your website.

User interviews are similar to focus groups, except that they are one-on-one meetings with individuals. You may want to schedule appointments with a broad range of current or potential users and ask them questions similar to what you would ask during a focus group.

The same principles will apply whether you conduct focus group or user interviews. You will benefit most by focusing on what you want to learn and paying attention to how participants describe things. Once you have compiled data that already exists about your audience, a combination of focus groups and user interviews may help fill in the gaps to develop the full picture.

Surveys and Feedback Forms

Surveys and feedback forms are also valuable as they allow users to share information with you directly and often result in both quantitative and qualitative data. Many libraries conduct regular LibQual or LibSat surveys, which can provide you with insight into user expectations and desires. You can also conduct website surveys, asking users who they are and what they are trying to do. Some online survey tools are available either for free or a small cost, including SurveyMonkey, Typeform, and Google Forms. In these survey tools, you can use logic features to ask specific questions of specific audience members.

Similarly, your library may solicit input in an ongoing way, allowing users to submit feedback, suggestions, or comments. This might be an online form made available through your website or comment cards placed at your service desks. These types of forms can ask specific questions to gather more quantitative data, or can be left open-ended to gather more qualitative data. Again, the type of data gathered in surveys and feedback forms can help further refine the definition of your audience and their primary tasks.

Web Analytics

Most likely, you collect analytics on your website through a tool such as Google Analytics or Siteimprove. If you don't collect analytics, you should. Web analytics are a great way to find out geographic and technical information about your users, such as

- Where they are located (city, country)
- What operating systems and versions they are using (Windows, Macintosh, iOS)
- What browsers they are using (Firefox, Chrome, Internet Explorer, Safari)
- What devices they are using (desktops, iPhones, iPads, Samsung Galaxy tablets)
- What content they accessing (individual web pages and sections of your website)

EXAMPLE OF USING SURVEY LOGIC

The first question can ask users to select their status (i.e., child, young adult, adult). Depending on the response given, users can be taken to a different set of questions. The questions for the children might ask about support for reading skills and homework help, whereas the questions for the adults can ask about support for their continuing education.

- How they are finding your website (search terms or referring websites)
- What web page they are landing on most often
- What keywords they are typing in the site search

As you look at analytics, be sure to look at data from at least the past year, since user behavior may vary depending upon the time of year. You may want to go back further, looking at several years, to best understand the trends.

Authors have written entire books on Google Analytics and how to use the data to help understand your users and guide your website decisions. For the purposes of defining your audience for usability testing, focus here on data that describes the usual behavior and primary tasks of your audience.

For instance, you may find out certain job help pages are accessed heavily. You can use this data to better describe the job-seeking audience segment. Similarly, you could find out which topic guides are used most regularly to identify subject areas of most interest to researchers. In table 3.1., you can see examples of heavily used web pages within an academic library and how this data might translate into a primary website tasks for your audience.

Site search data, often captured through web analytics, is a useful place to find out what terms actual users are searching on your website. For instance, you might find out that *software*, *fines*, and *e-books* are the most common search terms. You can translate search terms into primary tasks on your website, as demonstrated in table 3.2.

Anecdotal Data

Don't overlook qualitative, anecdotal data either. Public services staff members have regular, direct interaction with users and can share their stories with you. They can tell you what questions users regularly ask and where users struggle most. Bring together those people who interact with users directly, and gather their perceptions of users' backgrounds, goals, and common questions. After you have gathered data from a variety of other mechanisms, anecdotal data can be a helpful source both for confirming your assumptions and for filling in the gaps.

Table 3.1. Example of Translating Top Web Pages into Website Tasks

TOP WEB PAGE	POSSIBLE WEBSITE TASK
Newspaper Guide	Search for newspaper articles
Study Spaces	Reserve a study room
Databases A–Z	Find a specific database
Popular vs. Scholarly	Learn how to distinguish between popular and scholarly articles

Table 3.2. Example of Translating Search Terms into Website Tasks

TOP SEARCH TERM	POSSIBLE TASK
Software	Find out if a particular software is available on library computers
Fines	Find out about late fees or pay late fees
E-books	Locate e-books

⊚ Identify Your Primary Audience Segments

Once you have gathered enough data, you should be able to reasonably describe your primary audience along with their primary tasks. Keep in mind that your primary audience will not be just *one* type of individual. Libraries tend to serve a broad user base, and so you likely have several types of people who all fit within your primary audience.

The easiest way to describe an audience segment is by the key qualities that *distinguish them* from the other audience segments and will also distinguish them as far as user expectations, user needs, and user behavior. In a large academic library setting, your primary audience may include undergraduate students, graduate students, and faculty members, as demonstrated in table 3.3. In this case, the title of the audience segment reflects their status at the university. These distinctions make sense since undergraduate students may have less experience with library research and library services, but tend to be more comfortable using touch-screen and handheld devices. Graduate students have different needs and expectations related to the library, and faculty members have more familiarity with research databases that will cause their needs and behavior on the website to differ from the student population.

In a public library setting, your primary audience may include job seekers, young adult readers, and retirees. In this context, the title of the audience partially reflects their age as well as their needs related to the library, but it is easy to imagine that these audience segments would also have quite different expectations and behavior related to the website. In an archive or museum setting, your primary audience may include visiting researchers, historians, and tourists. Again, focus on the distinctions between the audience segments to develop the most helpful description of each segment.

It is a natural tendency to try and capture every type of person within your primary audience definition, but be cautious of doing this. If you have a base that is too broad, you will have a difficult time doing targeted recruitment as well as focusing on primary tasks for usability testing. If you find that over five distinct audience types are unavoidable to capture your primary audience, one method is to define secondary audience segments as well.

Another thing to consider is the difference between your actual primary audience and your target audience. It might be the case that you would like donors to be your primary audience, but in reality they make up a small proportion of your overall user base. While it is perfectly fine to focus some effort toward improving the user experience for target

Table 3.3. Example of Primary Audience Segments for an Academic Library

PRIMARY AUDIENCE SEGMENT	TECHNICAL KNOWLEDGE	SUBJECT KNOWLEDGE
Undergraduate students	• Use smartphones and tablets (usually iPhones and iPads) • Use the campus course management system (D2L or Blackboard)	• Not familiar with research databases • Not aware of interlibrary loan or document delivery services • Not aware of peer review
Graduate students	• Use laptops (usually Macs) • Use citation management systems	• Knowledgeable of particular journal titles • Knowledgeable of some research databases
Faculty members	• Use laptops and desktops • Not as comfortable with using smartphones	• Knowledgeable of databases in their particular discipline • Aware of journal impact factors

**EXAMPLE OF PRIMARY VS. SECONDARY AUDIENCES
FOR A UNIVERSITY'S SPECIAL COLLECTIONS**

Primary audience: faculty researchers, visiting scholars, graduate students
Secondary audience: tourists, school teachers, potential donors

audience members, be careful not to neglect those who are currently using your website most often.

Identify Tasks for Your Primary Audience Segments

After describing your primary audience segments, you can describe the primary tasks of each segment. Primary tasks are the tasks they most often attempt to complete on your website. Tasks can be very specific, such as "finding hours for a particular branch," but can also be broader, such as "researching a topic." As you developed your primary audience segments, you likely had some primary tasks in mind already. Continue to analyze the data you have gathered to best describe and refine the audience segments' primary tasks. Table 3.4 provides some example primary tasks associated with each previously established audience segment.

For example, if faculty members are one of your audience segments, you may take a closer look at a combination of instructional data, web analytics, and strategic planning documents. The instructional data might inform you that the most common request from teaching faculty is for classroom instruction from a librarian. Web analytics data might tell you that one of the most frequently clicked-on links from the "For Faculty" web page is "Request a Purchase." Strategic planning documentation may indicate that the need for digitization services has skyrocketed in the past year. Given this, you might develop the following primary tasks for the faculty audience:

Table 3.4. Example of Primary Tasks by Primary Audience Segment for an Academic Library

PRIMARY AUDIENCE SEGMENT	PRIMARY TASKS
Undergraduate students	• Search for books on a topic • Search for articles on a topic • Reserve a study room • Check out a laptop
Graduate students	• Search for an incomplete citation • Store and manage citations • Conduct a literature review • Request a long-term study room
Faculty members	• Request classroom instruction • Request items for purchase • Request digitization services • Locate journal impact factors • Search for grants • Store and manage research data

- Request classroom instruction
- Request items for purchase
- Request digitization services

You might find that you have a significant number of primary tasks for each audience segment. It is OK to have a substantial list of tasks, and it is possible that you will be able to test all of these tasks over time. Again, though, be cautious of trying to capture every possible example. By defining primary tasks in a thoughtful way based on data, you will be able to focus your efforts on the tasks most important to your audience, and therefore make usability improvements to your website that will have the largest impact.

⑥ Create Personas

A persona is a fictional character that represents the characteristics and the tasks of your primary audience and puts you in the mind of your user. It is a helpful activity to create personas in collaboration with your web team or with stakeholders, ensuring that everyone is in agreement about the audience members you are serving, their background, and what they are trying to do. Once developed, personas can be helpful to reference in an ongoing way at various points within a website effort. You can speak about personas as if they are real users of your website. Your personas can be shared broadly with library staff and stakeholders and brought into conversations when you are undergoing some conflict in opinion related to content, layout, or design. Personas can help you reach common ground and bring everyone's focus back on the user. They can serve as a helpful reminder to everyone that you are making decisions about your website based on the audience that the persona represents.

Since you have multiple primary audience segments, you will have multiple personas. Each persona should represent a segment of your audience, for instance, young adult reader, retiree, or single parent. Personas allow you to take the raw descriptions of your primary audience segments and translate them into realistic, relatable, and memorable characters.

Persona development requires you to be creative and use elements of storytelling. The personas you create should by nature be realistic because they will be based on actual data you have collected. To make each persona relatable, include a photograph of a real person and give each one a name. Avoid using stock images or cartoons, because you want the personas to seem as realistic and relatable as possible. Use storytelling to make the personas memorable, giving them character and personalities. If you find this challenging, you may want to identify a staff member who has a creative writing background and would be willing to help with this effort.

There is not an exact science to persona development and what content should or should not be included. You want to be descriptive enough to represent your audience, but succinct enough to be memorable. You can describe a persona with various types of content and can organize that content in different ways. You will probably want to include the most important and distinct characteristics of the particular audience segment. Perhaps you want to include demographic information, technology proficiency, relevant background knowledge, and relevant challenges.

The faculty member audience segment, for instance, is translated into a persona in figure 3.1.

Joel Isaac, Ph.D.

"I'm a big fan of the library and insist that my students use library resources in my class."

Why the University of Arizona?

I have been at Arizona since 2005 and am an Associate Professor. Before that I taught at Florida State. I did my undergraduate degree at Arizona and have family here.

How's Academic Life?

I teach several courses that have research components, including HIST 301: Introduction to the Study of History and HIST 396: Capstone Research Seminar. I have published 6 major papers since coming to the UA, mostly on cultural history within the Borderlands region. I plan to go up for full professor within the next two years.

Primary Tasks

Request classroom instruction

Joel is assigning his students a research paper, and wants to request a librarian conduct a classroom session on how to use library sources for primary research.

Request items for purchase

Joel's colleague in California recently published a book, and he wants the library to purchase a copy.

Fast Facts
- 38 years old
- History professor
- Enjoys browsing the stacks and using Special Collections

Technical Knowledge
- Uses his laptop on campus and in his office, desktop at home
- Doesn't have a smartphone and doesn't text, even though his kids keep nagging him about it

Subject Knowledge
- Comfortable using finding aids
- Familiar with JStor, Proquest Historical Newspapers, and Arizona Archives Online

Figure 3.1. Example of Persona for Faculty Member.

You can see that Dr. Joel Isaac is a history faculty member. He has a photograph and a quote that reflects his personality and goals. This particular persona includes fast facts and background information on why he works at the University of Arizona and what courses he is teaching. You can see that some of the data from table 3.1 and table 3.2 have been translated into Joel's characteristics: his technical knowledge, subject knowledge, and primary tasks. The primary audience segment is now represented not just with raw data, but with a character in the context of a story.

Personas are a helpful tool for many purposes. They encourage library staff members to get inside the mind of the user and make better, more user-centered decisions. They also become helpful in planning as you can translate persona scenarios into scenarios for usability testing.

Understand User Journeys

When describing your audience and preparing for usability testing, consider the entire user journey. This will give you greater contextual understanding of the user experience and its many aspects. User journeys include not just independent website tasks, but the entire context in which a user is visiting your website. Perhaps Joel uses his department page to access information about the library, rather than going to the library website directly. The department page links him to certain library web pages, such as the instructional request form, the history subject guide, or the history librarian's contact information. Perhaps he also has access to library services and resources through the course management system.

- *Request digitization services.* Mike has some historical newspapers and photographs he wants to digitize to use in his class. He wants to find out how much it costs and if there are any copyright restrictions.
- *Locate journal impact factors.* Annabelle is considering publishing in the journal *Climate Dynamics*, but wants to compare its impact factor to comparable journals in the field.
- *Search for grants.* Gabe wants to find grant funding to support his research project on student engagement.
- *Store and manage research data.* Yvonne secured National Science Foundation grant funding but needs to now put together a data management plan. She could use help planning for how to both store and manage her research data.

Similarly, Yvonne might start by checking the university website to find out about data management resources on campus, and Gabe may use Google to start his grant research.

In usability tests, facilitators usually ask participants to start on the home page and complete a given task. This is not always an authentic experience. For many website users, they do not start on the home page. They might begin their journey on Google or through a referring website. They might be directed to your website from a browser bookmark or a course management system. They may not land on the library's home page, but rather land directly on a web page deep within the structure of your website. Additionally, they might be accessing your website from their handheld device, with spotty Wi-Fi, or from off site where they will need to sign in before accessing any subscription materials.

Many surrounding factors will influence your users each time they try to use your website. Users do not access websites in a vacuum. So when defining your primary audience and their tasks, and when developing scenarios for usability testing, keep in mind not just your individual website, but the entire user journey that surrounds it.

⦿ Key Points

Understanding your audience segments and what they try to do on your website will help you create the most reliable and useful usability tests. Remember:

- A lot of data about your users already exists; you just need to fill in the gaps.
- Data should guide how you describe your primary audience segments and their primary tasks.
- You can develop personas to make your primary audience realistic, relatable, and memorable.
- Don't forget the entire user journey.

Now that you have a sense of your primary audience and their primary tasks, you are ready to begin planning for usability testing.

CHAPTER 4

Selecting a Method

Find out

▷ Why in-house, ongoing usability testing is in your best interests

▷ How the behavior of your audience will influence what type of usability testing you ought to conduct

▷ How your workflow, time frame, and available resources impact your options for usability testing

▷ When to organize which method of usability testing

As discussed in Chapter 2, usability testing can be conducted in house using resources that you either have already or that you can reasonably obtain. In this chapter, you will explore different types of usability testing and identify which method is right for your particular goals and context. The method most appropriate for your situation will vary depending on the availability of your primary audience as well as circumstances surrounding your current website efforts. You also may want to consider different methods at different moments within a particular web project. In most cases, you will want to organize a variety of testing methods over time, and build them into your ongoing plans for usability testing, which is covered in chapter 8.

In-House, Ongoing Usability Testing

Usability testing is not new to libraries, but it has often been either contracted out to a company or conducted only as a one-time or project-based effort. Some people tend to be fearful of in-house, or do-it-yourself, testing, since it might be time-consuming, expensive, and less reliable than if it was organized by professionals who do usability testing for a living. As discussed in chapter 2, however, usability testing is something that anyone has the ability to learn how to do, even with limited time and resources. The benefits of getting this experience and gaining these skills internally far outweigh any occasional risk of conducting invalid or unhelpful usability tests. By building the knowledge in-house, over time library staff members will recognize usability problems more quickly, solve usability problems more easily, and make better website decisions overall.

Further, conducting usability testing in an ongoing way is much more valuable than conducting it as a one-time effort. While it is undeniably valuable to conduct usability testing during a website redesign project, it should never end there. Usability testing should be part of an ongoing effort to improve your website. Rather than counting on website redesigns to fix all of your usability problems, you should strive for iterative, frequent improvements. User behavior changes often, including expectations and devices used. Web content is also regularly added and updated as new library services and resources are created or obtained. Ongoing usability testing will allow you to continually make improvements to your website, which is living, complicated, and ever changing.

To make this happen, you should find out how to conduct usability testing using human and technical resources that are regularly available to you. Ideally, you have a supporting structure and processes in place that will allow you the ongoing resources to conduct usability testing as needed for a variety of purposes—for a website redesign, for a new library service or resource—and in an ongoing way.

Sometimes it may be appropriate to contract out usability testing to professionals, and if you have the resources to do this regularly that can be of great value. However, this will likely never be a sustainable approach to *continually* improving the usability of your website. So no matter your situation, in-house, ongoing usability testing is the best method. But there are a number of methods that fall within this category, and the one appropriate for your situation will depend on a number of factors.

The Behavior of Your Primary Audience

A crucial component of successful usability testing is recruiting the right participants. Methods for discovering your primary audience are discussed in the previous chapter. Ideally, you want to conduct usability tests with participants who represent your primary audience or a particular segment of your primary audience.

However, what is most important is not that your participants fall neatly into your audience definition, but that their user behavior is representative of your primary audience. So, consider the uniqueness of the behavior of your primary audience. It is quite likely that you are able to recruit participants for your usability tests who won't perfectly match your primary audience, but who will match the *user behavior* of your primary audience. You just want the user behavior to be *close enough* to that behavior you would expect from your primary audience. A usability test with participants who have similar user behavior to your primary audience will undoubtedly provide you with useful results.

Technical knowledge: level of ability using technology

Functional knowledge: level of ability performing certain tasks or interactions

Domain knowledge: level of understanding of a particular topic or discipline

What is important is that participants have similar behavior to members of your actual audience. Your participants should approach a given scenario approximately the same way as you would expect your audience to, if they were in the same situation. Their behavior will be influenced by a number of factors, including comfort with technology, knowledge of services and terminology, and previous experience. This is where your audience definitions are especially useful. First, you should consider your primary audience's comfort level with particular technology, or their "technical knowledge." You may anticipate conducting usability tests on different devices with different operating systems, available browsers, and navigation elements. Consider if your audience is comfortable using

- Handheld and/or touch-screen devices to access websites, including typing, navigating, selecting buttons and links, and scrolling
- Different operating systems (e.g., Windows, Mac, iOS)
- Different browsers (e.g., Firefox, Internet Explorer, Chrome, Safari)

Further, you may want to include particular website tools or features as part of a usability test. Perhaps you would like the participants to chat with a librarian, submit a form, or search the catalog or a research database. You will again want to consider your audience's technical knowledge, but here you will also want to consider their "functional knowledge," or familiarity with particular web-based interactions. In these types of cases, consider how comfortable your audience is using

- Chat or instant messaging
- Request or feedback forms
- Search boxes or advanced search forms
- Facets, sorting, and other search refinement features

Also, you should consider their previous knowledge and familiarity with topics or concepts, often referred to as their "domain knowledge." In particular, you might want to test a website task that assumes some level of knowledge of a topic. Consider how familiar your audience is with

- Particular terminology
- A particular subject or research area
- Particular library services
- Particular information resources (e.g., databases, journals)
- Library research in general, and to what extent
- Searching library catalogs or research databases

You should be able to reasonably answer most of these questions about the primary audience segment you have in mind for a usability test. This will give you a sense of how

If testing a special collections website, consider your audience segment's level of domain and functional knowledge. Are they familiar with terminology such as *finding aids*, *primary sources*, *archives*, and *manuscripts*? Are they comfortable using a finding aid, browsing an online archive, or searching for primary documents?

unique their user behavior will be, and will help you determine what will be necessary for recruitment.

If you don't know enough to reasonably answer some of these questions, don't worry. It might be that your audience segment is diverse in its technological capabilities and knowledge. If this is the case, you may want to recruit participants who have a variety of capabilities to see if this has an impact on their behavior and success in completing tasks. You just need to be careful to not recruit only participants with higher levels of technical, domain, and functional knowledge, because your usability tests may not identify some significant usability problems for other users who fall within your primary audience.

In other cases, it might be that you simply don't have enough data to know your primary audience's level of knowledge. This is something you can work around, too. You can gather information to fill in the gaps as part of the usability testing session itself, by asking questions during the initial interview stage. Additionally, as you observe the participants attempting to complete tasks, you will gather anecdotal information that will help you understand their level of knowledge.

Once you have evaluated the knowledge of your primary audience, you should have a good idea about the uniqueness of their behavior. At this point, you may be able to broaden your audience scope for the purposes of recruiting participants for a usability test.

For example, a high school library may have teachers as a primary audience segment. Table 4.1 outlines an example of the technical, domain, and functional knowledge of this audience. While some characteristics are specific, such as familiarity with terminology, this level of knowledge overall is not particularly unique and may be similar across a broader audience. Perhaps school counselors, administrators, and parents would have similar levels of knowledge and comfort levels with different technology and topics. So while you would ideally recruit teachers, you could also recruit nonteachers who have similar levels of knowledge. In this case, you would broaden your possibilities for recruitment, making planning for usability testing a much easier process.

On the other hand, you may find that a particular audience segment will have unique behavior when it comes to completing tasks on your website. Table 4.2 outlines the knowledge of two other primary audience segment examples: visually impaired users and exhibition curators. In both cases, these audience segments have unique characteristics that may be difficult to find in a broader audience outside of these particular segments.

Visually impaired users may be fluent using JAWS Screen Reading Software, which is how they access your website content. Assuming you would expect participants to use this software during the usability test, you would need to find people with this particular level of technical knowledge. Exhibition curators are experienced with exhibition catalogs and finding aids. Assuming you are including a website task associated with exhibition catalogs or finding aids, you would need participants to have this level of functional knowledge.

Table 4.1. Example of Primary Audience Segment That Doesn't Have Unique Behavior

PRIMARY AUDIENCE SEGMENT	TECHNICAL KNOWLEDGE	DOMAIN KNOWLEDGE	FUNCTIONAL KNOWLEDGE
Teacher	• Comfortable using different operating systems and browsers • Less comfortable using handheld devices	• Familiar with terminology *interlibrary loan, databases* • Can read and interpret citations	• Experienced searching research databases • Used to communicating with chat and text messaging

Table 4.2. Example of Primary Audience Segments That Have Unique Behavior

PRIMARY AUDIENCE SEGMENT	TECHNICAL KNOWLEDGE	DOMAIN KNOWLEDGE	FUNCTIONAL KNOWLEDGE
Visually impaired users	• Comfortable with desktops or laptops, but not handheld devices • Fluent in using JAWS screen-reading software	• Comfortable searching library catalog • Rarely search library catalog	• Comfortable filling out a form but not using chat or instant messaging
Exhibition curators	• Comfortable with different devices and browsers	• Familiar with terminology *rights and reproductions, loans*	• Comfortable browsing exhibition catalogs • Experienced using finding aids

As you can imagine with these examples, the audience segments' technical, domain, and functional knowledge will influence their behavior when interacting with your website, and so you would be better off doing targeted recruitment of these audiences directly.

The Availability of Your Primary Audience

How you go about recruiting participants will depend significantly on their availability. Specifically, consider the following questions:

- Do you have an easy way to contact them?
- Are they physically near you, or at a distance?
- What are their schedules like? Do they work or go to school? Are they more available during the week or on the weekends?
- What is their mobility? Are they able to travel to your location easily, or do you need to go to them?

The answers to these questions will vary greatly depending on your audience and context. Fortunately for most libraries, members of your primary audience likely visit your physical facility, making them more readily available for contact and recruitment. For libraries located on college campuses, your audience is likely nearby even if they don't visit your actual building.

Reaching more specific audience segments, or audience segments that access your library only virtually, will require more thought and planning. Similarly, if you are at a virtual or closed-stack library, it may be more challenging to identify the availability of your audience and plan for recruitment.

More Targeted Testing

As alluded to earlier, the types of tasks on your website that you plan to test may influence what participants you should recruit. It might be the case that you are testing specific tasks that require not just a primary audience segment, but a more particular set of users within that audience segment.

For instance, you might be testing the usability of a service or tool that is geared toward a very particular type of user, such as an employment exploration tool geared toward job seekers, an archival research tool geared toward historians, or a study skills tutorial geared toward students with learning disabilities. In these types of cases, you will probably want to recruit participants who fall within those more specific audiences in order to get the most useful results from usability testing.

🌀 Your Time Frame, Workflows, and Goals

Time Frame

Time is obviously another important factor in planning for usability testing. If you have a strict deadline for launching a new website or implementing a particular new resource or service, you may need to recruit loosely and schedule several sessions over a short period of time. If you have a longer time frame, you can employ more targeted recruitment efforts and schedule sessions further in advance. As you develop strategies for ongoing usability testing, time becomes less of a challenge as it is built into your web team's schedule in a sustainable way.

Workflows

Any workflows or processes that you have in place associated with usability testing might also influence the method you select. You may not have any workflows in place currently, but they become necessary as you prepare for ongoing testing. Having established workflows and expectations around usability testing has a number of benefits. For example, your library might have a commitment to conduct usability testing on every substantial change to your website, including global navigation changes or changes to the home page. Similarly, your library might have a process for website redesign projects where in-depth usability testing sessions with members of each primary audience segment are an expectation before launch. More ideas on workflows and processes, and what these might look like at different institutions, are discussed in chapter 8.

Goals

The purpose of usability testing is, at its core, to discover usability problems so that you can fix them. Any method of usability testing can accomplish this. But there are often other goals associated with usability testing, and these can also influence which method is best for your situation.

One common goal of usability testing is to confirm that a change you made, or plan to make, improves your website's usability. Perhaps you discovered a usability problem in a previous test and are making a change that you believe will make it more usable, and want to confirm this by comparing it to the previous version. You might not have removed all usability problems associated with a particular task, but at least you want to ensure that you didn't make it worse, and that in fact you made it a bit easier. In this case, you might be happy with conducting just a couple of informal usability tests that confirm your assumption.

If a goal is to convince others of a usability problem,

- Recruit actual members of your primary audience
- Schedule longer sessions
- Use a (semi-)controlled environment
- Record your usability testing sessions

Another common goal of usability testing is to gather evidence to justify a decision. Perhaps you have discovered anecdotally that there is a problem with your website, but haven't been able to address the problem because you need to convince stakeholders of the need for change. You may plan to present your usability testing findings to library staff and administrators to convince them that a significant change ought to be made to your website. Your testing results may come under question, and so it is important to have quality data backing you up. In this case, it is probably best to give yourself more time, recruit more thoughtfully, conduct more usability tests, and record your usability sessions to use as evidence.

You may have other specific goals associated with a usability test, such as testing the accessibility of tutorials using screen readers, testing your new responsive design using an iPhone, or testing the functionality of a new room reservation app before the first day of classes. Again, consider your goals as you select a usability method. The participants you need to recruit, technology you need to use, and time frame you are working with might all be contributing factors.

⑥ Available Resources

Not surprisingly, human and financial resources are also important factors when it comes to identifying the method of usability testing that is right for you. While usability testing doesn't have to be expensive, as covered in chapter 2, your available budget will impact which usability testing method is most appropriate. If you are operating with a minimal, or nonexistent, budget, this will certainly limit your options for obtaining both technology and incentives. Fewer incentives or incentives with smaller value might mean that you will have difficulty recruiting participants for scheduled sessions that are longer in length. If you have a commitment from your library administration to fund usability testing, you may have more options for gaining substantial incentives, scheduling more and longer sessions, and purchasing recording software.

The availability of library staff is another factor. In an extreme case, you could be in a single-person library where usability testing is something you must do independently when you are able to find a spare moment. On the other hand, you might be the member of a larger user experience team that is dedicated to conducting usability testing as part of its work.

There are varied levels of resources required for different types of testing. Time to organize, staff resources required, and software and hardware costs and are all factors to consider.

⊚ Intercept versus Formal Recruitment

Intercept Recruitment

Advantages:

- It is easy and quick to organize.
- It requires few resources.
- It can be more authentic, since participants don't have time to prepare in advance.

Drawbacks:

- Your tasks and scenarios need to be quite simple.
- You will have less control over recruitment and participants.
- You will have less control over the environment.

One of the simplest ways to conduct usability testing is by recruiting participants informally at the time of testing. This method allows you to quickly organize testing as needed with minimal planning. Intercept usability testing is an on-the-fly method in which you recruit passersby to participate in your usability test. To do this, you might grab a laptop and set up a table and chairs in a busy location, such as a shopping center or college hall. If you work in a busy library building, you can probably conduct this testing on-site with actual library users. At the University of Arizona, intercept usability testing is conducted with students regularly from the main library lobby.

The beauty of intercept usability testing is that it is flexible as far as location and timing, and it can be very quick to organize. This works well if you are on a short time frame, you have just a few tasks to test, and your audience is easily available. Intercept usability testing is a great method to include in your plan for ongoing usability testing. It can be used for quick tests of small, incremental changes.

Additionally, this method can be a bit more authentic than formally scheduled testing, because the participants are not expecting to complete tasks and have no time to prepare in advance. It is possible with scheduled testing that participants look at your website beforehand, review the content, and consider what they might say during the test.

There are limitations to the intercept method of testing, though. You will have less control over who you are able to recruit and therefore who ends up actually participating in the test. It is therefore less useful if your primary audience has distinct characteristics and is not easily available. Intercept testing also might not work well if you have more substantive tasks to test. Because you are asking participants to unexpectedly take time out of their day, you should not expect them to sit with you for much longer than a few minutes. You also may find that they are less patient during the test and less willing to talk through their process in a thoughtful manner.

Formal Recruitment

Advantages:

- You will be able to do more targeted recruitment of particular audience segments.
- You will be able to test more specific or in-depth tasks and scenarios.

Drawbacks:

- It requires more staff time for recruitment and scheduling.
- It usually requires a higher level of funding for incentives.

More formal, structured usability testing involves scheduling appointments in advance. One of the great benefits of this method is that you can do more precise recruitment of members of your primary audience. You can also usually facilitate longer sessions, perhaps spending an hour or more with a single participant. It is also a more predictable structure and you can better control the environment. You can use a quiet, dedicated usability testing room with a desktop computer, comfortable furniture, and any associated hardware such as a webcam and microphone.

The drawback of formal recruitment is that, not too surprisingly, it requires more resources. Targeted recruitment can take more thought and effort, as can scheduling appointments and communicating with participants. You will likely require more substantive incentives than you would for impromptu, intercept testing, since you are asking participants to schedule time out of their day. You also run the risk of a participant not showing up at their appointment time, requiring that you reschedule or have a back-up participant on call.

⑥ In-the-Lab versus In-the-Field Testing

In-the-Lab Testing

Advantages:

- You have more control over the environment.
- It will usually be easier logistically.

EXAMPLE CASE STUDY: INTERCEPT VERSUS SCHEDULED TESTING FOR A SPECIAL COLLECTIONS WEBSITE

At the University of Arizona, the project team that was redesigning the Special Collections website initially used intercept recruitment with candy bars as the incentive. The first round was conducted in front of the main library with a project team member's smartphone, simply recruiting passersby to participate. Later, testing was conducted using a table and laptop setup in front of Special Collections. In both cases, they found out quite quickly that the previous knowledge and expectations of the volunteer student and library staff participants did not match that of the primary audience. They were able to still gather some useful data, but decided more targeted recruitment was necessary. Subsequently, they scheduled one-hour usability testing sessions with members of their primary audience: undergraduate history students, graduate students, faculty members, and archivists. For this formal recruitment, they used $25 gift cards as incentives. These sessions were more in-depth and were recorded using the Silverback software. Results from the scheduled sessions provided more substantive input and allowed the project team to better focus efforts on addressing the more authentic usability problems that were discovered.

Drawbacks:

- You need a lab location that is easy for participants to get to.
- It is less authentic than testing in the field.

Scheduled usability testing is most commonly conducted on-site, in a controlled environment such as a library meeting room, library workstation, or perhaps in a dedicated usability testing lab. This allows you to have control over the technology and the environment, and is relatively easy to organize and schedule since it is within your workplace. Yet, it is not the most authentic environment for ensuring realistic behavior by participants.

In-the-Field Testing

Advantages:

- It may allow you to discover usability problems you wouldn't discover otherwise.
- It is more authentic than testing in the lab.

Drawbacks:

- It can be difficult logistically.
- It may require more resources for traveling outside the workplace.

Alternatively, you can conduct testing where you don't ask the user to come to you: you go to where the user is. If you are using intercept recruitment, it may just be a matter of going to the library lobby, the student union, a local park, or a shopping center. Essentially, you go to a busy location and approach participants to volunteer for testing. Intercept testing that is in the field requires less equipment, since you won't need a table, chairs, or dedicated testing space. It also gives you some more flexibility since you can move locations as needed to find more participants. At the University of Arizona, the facilitator and note taker often just walk to the student union to conduct testing with students who have a few spare moments.

Intercept, in-the-field testing is a good option, but prepare for these types of sessions to be shorter, since participants might be standing or on the move. Also consider the logistics. If you are using a laptop, you will need to have a table and/or seats available. This works well in a food court, train station, or study hall, but might not work well on a busy walkway. A tablet or smartphone allows for more flexibility since a participant can hold and use the device standing up without a table.

Recruiting in advance and scheduling appointments for in-the-field testing is a less common method, but has a number of advantages. This testing method might involve going to a faculty member's office, a student's dorm room, a teacher's classroom, or a retiree's home. This can be challenging logistically, and may require extra costs in both staff time and any travel expenses. Yet, this can be one of the most authentic methods since you are observing users in their natural environment. This can provide you with insight into the broader user journey and can make you aware of stumbling blocks users might encounter because of an environmental issue you hadn't previously considered.

⊚ Local Technology versus Participants' Technology

Local Technology

Advantages:

- You can control the device, operating system, or browser used during the test.
- You can use recording software more easily.
- You will have more controlled usability tests over multiple sessions.
- You can test a website that is in the development stage and only available locally.

Drawbacks:

- It is less authentic than using participants' technology.
- You may not discover usability problems that exist when using other technology.

In most cases, people conduct usability tests using their local technology. The organizer usually has a computer, whether it is a desktop, laptop, or handheld device. This is sometimes a necessity if you are testing a website that is in development and couldn't be accessed from a participant's personal device. It also allows you to use any locally installed software, such as screen-recording software. If you are organizing several usability testing sessions, it allows the experience to be more controlled, giving you more scientific and comparable results from one session to the next.

Logistically, using your own technology is much easier. Yet, there are instances where it can be worthwhile to consider the alternative.

Participants' Technology

Advantages:

- It is more authentic than using local technology.
- It may allow you to test elements of the broader user journey.
- You can discover problems associated with different technology being used.

Drawbacks:

- It can be more difficult logistically.
- It requires that participants have personal devices easily available.
- It may only work for audiences who carry their devices with them.

In the real world, users are accessing your website from a myriad of devices with various operating systems, screen sizes, and browser versions. By only testing with local, controlled technology, you may miss usability problems that are prevalent out in the real world. Because of this, it can at times be a good option to use participants' technology instead of your own.

For instance, if you ask participants to bring up a browser, giving them no particular direction, you may find that they use a browser version you don't usually test, such as

Internet Explorer in compatibility mode. This may cause you to discover problems with the rendering of your menu navigation, footer, or other website elements. Further, you might find that your website is problematic if JavaScript is disabled, if the Internet connection is slow, or if Flash or Java need upgrading.

Using participants' technology can be particularly helpful if one of your goals of testing relates to accessibility using different technology, or if you would like to explore more of the user journey. If you are organizing a session with a visually impaired participant, for instance, you would likely gather more authentic results if the participant uses his or her own machine, software, and hardware. If you are organizing a session to test your mobile app, you may ask the participant to first download it to his or her personal device, testing the broader experience without assuming the user will have the app already installed.

In-Person versus Remote Testing

In-Person Testing

Advantages:

- It is usually easier both logistically and technically.
- It is easier to facilitate.

Drawbacks:

- It is more difficult to reach audience members who are at a distance.
- It is more difficult to recruit audience members who lack availability.

In-person testing is the most common approach, and in most cases, in-person testing is your best option. It doesn't require software, is logistically more straightforward, and allows you to easily play the role of facilitator during the session, encouraging participants to speak out loud and verbalize their experience.

Remote Testing

Advantages:

- It makes it easier to recruit participants who are at a distance.
- It can be more authentic since participants will be using their local computer.

Disadvantages:

- It can be more difficult both logistically and technically.
- It can be more difficult to facilitate.

In some outlying cases, your audience might be physically inaccessible to you—for instance, if you work at a virtual library that is serving a distant population, and that population has distinct characteristics that make it unique from the population that is readily available to you.

Fortunately, usability testing can be conducted remotely. A remote usability test will allow participants to take part in a test from their own local computer. Remote testing can be moderated in real time or can be facilitated entirely through technology.

Moderated Remote versus Unmoderated Remote Testing

Moderated Remote Testing

Advantages:

- You can facilitate the test in real time.
- You can observe the test in real time.

Drawbacks:

- It can be more difficult to schedule participants who lack availability.

Moderated, synchronous testing can be achieved remotely using a videoconference or virtual meeting tool, such as Skype, Adobe Connect, Blackboard Collaborate, GoTo-Meeting, or Google Hangouts. These tools allow participants to share their screens with you in real time, so you can see their interactions live as you would during an in-person test. You can also communicate directly with participants using a microphone. By using one of these tools, you have the advantage of acting as a facilitator in real time. Depending on the software you use, you may also be able to record the session for later viewing.

You may run across technical challenges at first, but real-time testing it is usually the best option if you need to conduct testing remotely. It allows you to mimic an in-person usability test and has all of the same advantages.

Unmoderated Remote Testing

Advantages:

- You can have participants complete the testing on their own schedule.
- It requires less staff time in scheduling and facilitating.

Drawbacks:

- You are unable to facilitate or observe the test in real time.
- It can be challenging for participants with less technical knowledge.
- It can be difficult both logistically and technically.
- You may have failed tests that don't give you any useful data.

Alternatively, you can use specialty software that will allow participants to take part in the test at a time that is convenient to them. This is an unmoderated, asynchronous variation on usability testing where the results will be recorded for your later viewing and analysis. This is a helpful option if your audience has limited availability, making the scheduling of appointments difficult. It can also be helpful if you would like to reach a large number of participants, since it does not require scheduling or facilitation time on the part of library staff. Several software options are available that provide this service, including OpenHallway and Loop11.

Unmoderated remote testing has some challenges. For one, you do not have a live facilitator to conduct the test, ask the participant questions, and keep the test moving along. Second, the participant may have to judge whether he or she has completed a particular task based on the scenario that was provided. Third, again, not having a facilitator, the participant has no one to whom he or she can ask questions. You rely solely on instructions relayed through the tool in order for the participant to understand the test. Some participants may not read the instructions carefully and may not understand the purpose of the test or how to go about completing it. Because of this, asynchronous testing works best when your audience has high technical and functional knowledge to understand and follow the directions.

So if you are planning for unmoderated usability testing, keep these tips in mind:

- Have very clear instructions, both within your recruitment message and within the tool itself.
- Test the scenarios thoroughly before you recruit, making sure they are completely understandable to an average user.
- Pilot the remote testing experience with colleagues or actual users prior to broader recruitment. This will ensure that your instructions are clear.
- You may get results that are not useful, in which the participants did not understand the scenario or how to participate in the test correctly. Because of this, it is useful to recruit a larger number of participants than you might normally.

Key Points

There is no ideal method for conducting usability testing, since each variation has its own advantages and disadvantages. You should select the method that is most appropriate for you given your particular situation. Remember:

- There is no excuse for *not* conducting your own, in-house usability testing.
- The behavior and the availability of your primary audience, as well as your time frame, workflows, and goals for testing, are determining factors in selecting a method.
- You have many methods to choose from and will probably use different methods at different times for different purposes.

Now that you know the various approaches to testing, it is time to actually plan out the logistics of usability testing.

Planning a Usability Test

BEFORE CONDUCTING A USABILITY TEST, you need to plan for who, what, when, where, and how. You need to write scenarios that reflect the tasks you want to test, and organize the people, technology, and other resources that will be required. Depending on the type of testing you are conducting, this planning phase can take a few weeks or just a few minutes.

Identify a Facilitator and Note Taker

There are two key elements to running a successful usability test: good facilitation and good note taking. Usually, a facilitator leads the usability test, giving directions to the participant and keeping things moving along. This is a requirement for any real-time testing, whether it is in person or remote. The facilitator for a given usability test should ideally be involved in all the planning stages, including the creation and piloting of the scenarios before the actual event. This will ensure that he or she is familiar with the content of the test and is comfortable when the time comes to walk participants through it. Running these tests can take some practice, and some guidelines for good facilitation will be discussed in chapter 6.

It is helpful to also have a note taker who can capture what happens during the usability test. This is especially important if you are not planning to record the usability test in any other way. A note taker requires less knowledge and training than a facilitator, but does need to have good listening skills and be able to capture notes quickly and legibly. The note taker should be trained beforehand in how to take effective notes to ensure that the most useful information is recorded. In general, you will want the note taker to capture

- Participant information
- Task(s) the participant is asked to complete
- Details of each attempt the participant makes to complete each task
- Number of attempts the participants makes
- If the participant ultimately succeeds or fails in completing the task(s)
- Any interesting comments the participant makes during the process

Details and examples of effective note taking are given in chapter 6.

Decide What to Test

Test What Is Most Important

Library websites tend to be quite complex, so you likely won't be able to test tasks that cover their every aspect. Rather, you need to focus on testing the things that are most important to your audience. Fortunately, by establishing primary tasks in chapter 3, you should have a good sense of what tasks you want to focus on for usability testing. By focusing your effort on what is most important to your users, you will be able to identify usability problems that have the most impact and address them as quickly as possible.

Consider Your Goals

As discussed in chapter 4, the type of usability testing you select may well depend on the goals of your test. Similarly, what tasks you test will also depend upon your goals at the time.

If you are just beginning to conduct testing on your website, you will want to focus on the primary tasks as defined in chapter 3. If you have more specific goals or an area of focus, such as a new discovery tool or a redesign of a particular section of your website, you will want to establish tasks specific to that area of focus.

Test What You Have Control Over

The main purpose of conducting a usability test is to act on the results: to make improvements to your website. Because of this, you are going to want to primarily test the things that you have control over. Most of your general web pages will be under your library's control, and users will likely be able to complete many of your primary tasks by using just your regular library web pages. Such tasks may include finding out what hours the library is open, how to get a library card, or how to register for an event. These types of basic tasks are the easiest things to test, and they are probably your best choice when you first get your feet wet with usability testing. If you discover usability problems while testing these types of tasks, you can usually implement solutions relatively quickly.

That said, a number of library website tasks are more complicated than this. Primary tasks will often require users to interact with web products or tools that are managed externally and that you have less control over. For instance, your tasks may involve your library's web-based discovery tool, catalog, databases, or interlibrary loan system. This doesn't mean that you can't test those important tasks; it just means that you need to be aware of limitations and consider how to best focus the tasks so that you get actionable results. So as you select tasks for usability testing, consider what type of changes you will be able to make as a result of what you find out. It can be frustrating to discover usability problems that you subsequently cannot address.

Keep in mind that even if you discover usability problems that you don't have the capability of fixing yourself, you do have the ability to suggest solutions to the people who do. This might be a vendor that provides a commercial product, or a web development

WHAT ABOUT TESTING SEARCH FUNCTIONALITY?

Focusing on what you have control over can be especially difficult for libraries, since many primary tasks relate to *searching*, yet libraries don't tend to actually manage the entire search functionality or design in house. Libraries most often rely on outside vendors, and while some customization is usually possible, it has limitations.

The good news is that for search-related tasks, you do have a lot of control on the design and implementation of initial access points. This includes design of the search forms, including any tabs, labels, or buttons, as well as size and location within the web page. You also have control over how you describe and present search options from your website, and how well you do at leading users in the most useful direction for their particular research need.

With many search tools, you will also have control over pre-limiting facets, which will customize what results appear by default. For instance, you may discover that excluding book reviews or news articles, or limiting results to items owned by your library will help with the usability of the search results.

You may also have some control within the user interface itself. Perhaps you can provide help resources, using contextual help or help at point of need. You likely have some control over your link resolvers and how full-text access or interlibrary loan options are presented to the user. You may also have the ability to encourage users to give you feedback when they encounter issues within a database. How this type of feedback is presented and encouraged might be within your control.

So while searching tasks are rarely entirely within your control, you usually have some ability to make changes. If searching is a primary task on your website, it is probably worth testing. The results will help you make smart customization choices and improve their usability, even within known limitations.

community that supports an open source product. With usability testing results in hand, you will be more likely to convince the powers that be of any usability problems and justify the need for addressing them.

So while you should focus most of your usability testing efforts on problems you can actually address directly, don't avoid testing externally controlled systems altogether. Usability testing results can make a strong case for change, and you can provide feedback to the people who have the ability to do something about it.

ⓢ Write Tasks and Scenarios

Task: what you want them to do (for internal purposes)

Scenario: what you tell them to do (for participant)

Write Tasks

For each item you have participants go through during a usability test, you should have a task and a scenario. The task is what you actually want them to complete, and the scenario is what guides them to completing that task. So to plan for the actual facilitation of a usability test, you need to start by creating a list of tasks.

Write out the tasks you want to test in simple language. These might be identical or similar to the primary tasks you defined in chapter 3. The best way to phrase the task is in a way that would allow you to clearly indicate "success" or "failure" associated with the task. The test participant will not see the actual task, and so it is OK to use labels or jargon if it is appropriate. Remember that the purpose of the tasks is for you to clearly document what you are testing and to track success and failure rates. You never actually share the tasks with the participants. Example tasks are

- Find library hours
- Request an interlibrary loan
- Find a book title in the catalog

Some tasks will be more complicated than others and will vary in complexity depending on your website or services offered. Be sure to clearly define what success would mean, as this will help you in making sense of your tasks and what you are trying to find out. Attempting to complete the task yourself on the website will help with this activity, as you can confirm what success actually might look like in context. It might be that there are several paths that could lead to success, and that's OK. By defining *success* in specific terms, you will know with confidence if the user has completed the task.

Table 5.1 includes examples of tasks and how success might be defined. As you can see, the definition of *success* can be quite specific, such as downloading a file or reading and understanding a particular piece of content. This level of specificity can be helpful during the test itself: the note taker will know when to mark down "success," and the facilitator will know when it is time to move on to the next task.

You will often discover that you need to think about specifics associated with a task. If you attempt to complete the task on your website, you may find that what was one initial

Table 5.1. Example of Tasks and Success Measures

ORIGINAL TASK	MORE SPECIFIC TASK	DEFINITION OF SUCCESSFUL COMPLETION
Find library hours	Find closing hours for the Main Library on Saturday	Find out the Main Library is open until 9 p.m. this coming Saturday
Find floor maps	Find and download a floor map for the Main Library	Download PDF of Main Library, Floor 1
Request an interlibrary loan	Request a book through interlibrary loan	Fill out and submit the "Request a Book Loan" form

primary task actually translates into two or more tasks for testing. For instance, "Find library hours" might not be specific enough, since this could mean a number of different thing, such as finding

- Hours for a particular library branch
- Hours for today, in the future, or for a particular day of the week
- Opening and closing hours
- Hours for the public versus hours for library members or affiliates

So in table 5.1, while the original primary website task was "Find library hours," the more specific task variation is finding hours for a particular location on a particular date. Perhaps this variation was selected because this is a very common question, and if users can find this information they can likely find comparable information for the different branches.

Similarly, "Find floor maps" could have a number of variations, such as

- Finding a map of a particular floor
- Finding a particular type of content within the floor maps, such as restrooms and elevators
- Finding where a particular service desk or office number is located

As you can imagine, each variation would have different success measures. In table 5.1, the variation chosen is finding the map of a particular floor. The reason for this is that the goal of the usability testing is to make sure the maps are findable, not to interpret content within the maps themselves.

Finally, "Request an interlibrary loan" might also include several possible tasks, such as requesting a book, article, or film. It may also involve making a request from a system, such as a discovery tool, or it might be making a request based on a written citation. In some libraries, you might have different forms or processes associated with these different versions of a task. So consider what you are really trying to test and be as clear as possible. In table 5.1, the variation chosen is the one where the participant fills out and completes the book request form without going through the discovery tool or another system.

As you go through the process of thinking more critically about the tasks you want to test and how you would measure success, you may find that you want to test all of the variations of a broader task. This might mean creating a number of usability testing tasks out of what was originally just a single task. If you struggle with this and end up with a large list of related tasks, you might find it helpful to step back and, again, consider what is most important, consider your goals, and consider what you have the power to fix.

IS IT BETTER TO HAVE A LOT OF TASKS OR JUST A FEW?

For less controlled testing, which is the focus of this book, it is better to have too many tasks on your initial list than too few. This way, you will get the most out of your time with each participant, covering a higher number of tasks and getting more insight into your website's usability strengths and failures.

You can always remove tasks once you realize it will take too long to complete them all. You may also find out quite quickly that one of the tasks is either very easy to complete, with 100% success rate, or nearly impossible to complete, with a 0% success rate. When this happens, you will be better off removing the task from your list for the time being. For the successful tasks, there is no need to continue testing if it is clearly an easy thing for all participants to do. For the difficult tasks, you might need to make an improvement to your website and then test again, or rethink the task altogether. There is no need to continue to test a task that nobody can complete.

This is something you can work on as you are creating the tasks, but it also might be something that comes up as a question once you begin to translate your tasks into actual scenarios for testing. You may find that creating clearly defined tasks can be a bit confusing and challenging at times, but this is to be expected. It is not worth worrying about too much, and it's OK if you don't get things perfect the first time. You can always adjust things later.

Another area you may struggle with is determining how many tasks to include in a particular test. Depending upon the method of testing you are planning for, you can have anywhere from 1 to 15 tasks. As you determine how many tasks and scenarios to include in a particular test, consider the time you have allocated and the complexity of each task. Ideally, you want to make sure that you can cover all of the tasks in a single usability testing session. Again, be flexible and understand that things may have to be adjusted as you move along.

Translate Tasks into Scenarios

Once you have your list of tasks, you will need to translate the tasks into scenarios. The scenario is what you will instruct the participant to do. It guides the participant toward completing an actual task without instructing them to do it directly. The goal is to make the scenarios realistic and non-leading. You will actually read out loud and/or give the written scenario to the participant, so the language you use can be very important.

Scenarios might reflect a single task or they might reflect multiple, related tasks. Table 5.2 demonstrates how original examples of primary tasks from chapter 3 can be first translated into tasks for usability testing, and then translated into scenarios for usability testing.

Write Clearly

You need to make sure your scenarios are as clear, direct, and unambiguous as possible. For instance, if you ask faculty members to "request items for their class," they may in-

Table 5.2. Examples of Tasks Translated into Tasks and Scenarios

PRIMARY TASK OF AUDIENCE	TASKS FOR USABILITY TESTING	SCENARIO FOR USABILITY TESTING
Check out a laptop	• Find out what laptops are available • Find out how to check out a laptop	Your laptop crashed last night. Find out if you can check out a Mac from the library and for how long.
Request a long-term study room	• Find out eligibility for long-term study rooms • Submit a "Request a Long-Term Study Room" form	Your adviser told you the library has quiet rooms for grad students that you can use for a whole year. Find out if you are eligible and if so, apply for a room.
Request items for purchase	• Find the "Suggest a Purchase" form • Submit a "Suggest a Purchase" form	The library doesn't have the latest edition of the *Associated Press Stylebook*. Request that the library order this book.

terpret this to mean place items on reserve, request holds, request purchases, or request digitization. Be sure to include any context that is necessary so that participants don't have room for interpretation. This will both keep the usability study more controlled and prevent participants from either getting confused or having to ask clarifying questions of the facilitator.

Be Specific

Further, you need to make sure the scenarios are specific, including any detail that is necessary. For instance, if you are asking participants to reserve a room, what time should they reserve it for? How many people are in the group? If this information is necessary to complete the task, include that information in the scenario rather than having participants guess at it or ask you about it during the test. Again, this will make things easier on both the participants and the facilitator, and will make for a more controlled test across different participants and sessions.

Allow Participants to Contribute

At the same time, you may want to allow participants some flexibility, encouraging them to bring in their own ideas to fill in the details of the scenario. This has the benefit of keeping the test authentic by ensuring the task is something the person might *actually do* out in the real world. This can lead to more helpful results as well as results you might not come across otherwise. It further has the benefit of motivating the participant to complete the task successfully. If the participant is not at all interested in the task at hand, he or she might be less likely to put effort and energy into completing it.

For example, if you are testing your library catalog, you might give participants some parameters (e.g., keyword or title search only) but then ask them to search for a topic that is of interest to them. Similarly, you might ask them to find an upcoming library exhibit they would be interested in visiting.

Keep in mind, though, that this needs to be a balance. You want the scenario to be direct and unambiguous so that participants understand the intent, while also giving them some leeway to fill in the gaps. Scenarios that are too broad can confuse participants and lead them to misunderstand the goal of the task.

BETTER SCENARIOS ARE DIRECT AND UNAMBIGUOUS

Scenario: You professor requires that you find scholarly articles for your research paper. Find scholarly articles that support your research interests.

Better scenario: Your professor requires that you have at least one scholarly article for your research paper. Find one scholarly article about the Obama presidency that interests you.

Be especially careful with having participants add their own details if you are trying to gather data to make a case for change. While you want participants to choose some of the details where it makes sense, you don't want to lose control of the test and subsequent results, making those results more difficult to interpret and act upon later.

Be Non-Leading

Perhaps the most important thing is to be careful that your scenarios are not leading in any way. Avoid using library jargon, such as *catalog*, *reference*, and *interlibrary loan*. Also avoid using terms that are identical to menu items in your primary navigation.

Watch out for trigger words: those words that will cause a user to select a particular link or go down a particular navigation path. If you include "research guides" in your scenario, for instance, the participant might immediately scan the website for the phrase "research guides," even if this isn't what he or she would do in real life. This is especially

**IMPROVING SCENARIO WORDING TO AVOID
TRIGGER WORDS AND PHRASES**

When you initially write scenarios, you might be tempted to keep things simple with wording such as

- Find digitization services.
- Submit a video streaming request form.
- Find children's programming.

While concise, these types of scenarios often lead the participant because they will focus in on the unique terms or short phrases: *digitization services*, *video streaming*, and *children's programming*. They will spend time looking for those specific words within the navigation and content of your website.

Better scenarios put the participant in context and are more descriptive. The previous scenarios can be reworded to be more effective:

- You need to digitize a document. Find out how.
- You need to request a video to be streamed for your course. How would you do this?
- You want to see what events the library organizes for children. What can you find out on the website?

problematic if you have a label in your navigation with the exact title "Research Guides." By including this phrase in the scenario, you are leading the participant to select that particular navigation item. So be cautious of this.

Trigger words can be problematic even if the term or phrase isn't included in the navigation. Words you use in your scenario are very important, and you might accidentally use language that makes participants think they need to look for a particular keyword, label, or term on your website. To help alleviate this issue, avoid specific noun phrases, replacing them with more descriptive text.

Be Concise

While keeping all of these things in mind, you also need to try to keep your scenarios concise and to the point. Only use language that is essential. Don't include unnecessary explanation or get too creative in storytelling. You don't want to distract the participants or cause them any confusion.

Spend time writing good scenarios to reflect the tasks you want to test, and keep in mind that even a slight difference in wording can lead to different results. Once you think your scenarios are ready, read them out loud a few times to colleagues to see if they make sense. You also will benefit from doing a short test run beforehand to see if there are any issues with your wording so that you can make adjustments before the actual usability test.

⑥ Order the Scenarios

If you are testing more than one scenario during a usability testing session, you will need to consider the order in which to read the scenarios. In some cases, the order will be an

SIMPLIFYING WORDING IN A SCENARIO

You want your scenarios to be as easy to understand as possible. While adding detail can help with this, it can also lead to long-winded scenarios that are hard for participants to follow. Cutting fluffy content or unnecessary words can help with this. For example, you might have a task that reads, "Reserve a study room for two people." You avoid using the word *reserve*, since this is a word within your menu navigation. So, you might start with a scenario written as

> You need to find a study room in the main library for yourself and a friend who need to work on a history project for a class you're currently taking. Find out if a main library study room is available and how you can book it.

There is information within this scenario that isn't necessary. The fact that it is a history project isn't relevant, and the fact that it is a current class is a given. It is also mentioned twice that the location is the main library. So, to simplify, this scenario could be re-written as

> You need to find a room in the main library for yourself and a friend to work on a project. Find out if a study room is available and how to book it.

EXAMPLE OF TRANSLATING A TASK INTO A SCENARIO

Let's say you want to test if users can find your library newsletter, *Library Currents*. On the website, there is a link titled "*Library Currents* (PDF)." One of the tasks you want to test is if users can find and open up the PDF of the latest newsletter. The task is "Find the PDF newsletter from last month." The task is successfully completed if the participant downloads the PDF of the December newsletter.

You need to think of a scenario in which someone would want to see this newsletter, and then write it in a clear way that is non-leading. So, the scenario is "Your friend told you there is a good article in the library's most recent newsletter. See if you can find the newsletter."

Notice what is and is not included in this scenario. It does not include leading or unnecessary information, and it does not include information that might complicate the task beyond the goal of the test. So, it does not include

- Jargon or trigger words, such as *Library Currents* or PDF
- The detail that the newsletter will need to be downloaded
- The title of the article that was recommended

Yet, it does include context and what is necessary to complete the task:

- The context of why they would look for the newsletter in the first place (to find a good article recommended by a friend)
- Which specific newsletter they want

---

obvious decision because your tasks build upon each other. In other cases, you will have a variety of options for ordering, but will need to keep in mind some other issues that may impact the results of the test.

Scenarios That Have a Set Order

If your tasks build upon each other, the order in which to read them might be obvious. For instance, if you are conducting a test of a search tool, you may have a number of tasks that need to be completed in a particular order. Perhaps the tasks involve typing an initial search query, refining a search, selecting a search result, and so on. In this case, your order will be obvious and you won't have much flexibility.

This type of usability test can be a bit problematic, since the order of the scenarios may be a bit inauthentic and not represent the true experience of an actual user. Participants are also going to be gaining knowledge of the process along the way, as you guide them to the next step with your subsequent scenarios. To help alleviate this issue, you may want to do a number of variations on this type of test, tweaking the scenarios and occasionally starting the usability test in the midst of the process rather than from the beginning. You can also write a more complicated scenario that involves the different pieces but doesn't specify an order in which the participant is to complete them, allowing the participant to interpret the steps more naturally.

To be clear, this doesn't mean that you shouldn't conduct this type of usability testing. It is just a limitation to be aware of and consider as you plan for testing and then later analyze your results.

Scenarios That Are Independent of Each Other

In most cases, you are going to be ordering scenarios that are not dependent on one another and therefore don't require a particular order. What is important to keep in mind in these cases is that participants will still gain knowledge and experience as they attempt to complete each task, and this may influence their ability to complete subsequent tasks. Especially if you are testing related or similar tasks, this has the ability to skew your results. This is an important consideration, since you might not discover legitimate usability problems related to a task if the participants gain related knowledge during an earlier task. This knowledge tends to be related to navigation or content, so by attempting to complete one task, a participant gains understanding of navigation elements and/or exposure to relevant content.

Fortunately, there are a few things you can do to minimize this problem. In many cases, tasks can be conducted completely independently of one another, which allows you to randomize the order for each participant. If you conduct enough tests, this randomization ought to catch any usability problems that might be missed when the tasks are completed in a particular order.

Additionally, you can try to make sure that your tasks in a given session are either minimally related or not related whatsoever. For instance, you can make sure that you are not asking participants to complete multiple tasks associated with one particular section of the website or one particular tool. This won't be realistic in some cases, particularly on smaller websites, but it is something to keep in mind when possible.

If nothing else, be sure to pay close attention during each test to notice if someone's behavior is being impacted by the experience they had with previous tasks. As the participants speak out loud about their experience and decision making, you may notice where they are gaining knowledge and how this might be impacting their behavior. More about how to interpret user behavior and comments will be discussed in chapters 6 and 7.

Realize that there are limitations to the results of usability testing, and the knowledge that participants gain during the process of usability testing is one of them. It is a consideration and something to keep in mind during the analysis phase.

Decide When to Test

For all real-time usability testing, you will need to set aside some time in your schedule to conduct the tests. The best time will vary depending on your method of testing and other circumstances.

For intercept testing, especially as you plan for ongoing testing, consider the best time of year, day of the week, and time of day. Again, consider your audience and their behavior. Factors for time of year might include

- Weather
- Holidays, summer or winter vacations
- Final exams

The day of the week and time of day might be relevant, too. If your audience members are students on a college campus, you may have better success in having volunteers if you conduct the testing during the regular school or work week in the afternoons. If your audience members are working parents, evenings and weekends might be a better option. So when considering the best time, keep in mind

- Work schedules
- School schedules
- Other commitments or special events (e.g., sports games, graduations, festivals)

For intercept testing, you may want to block off an hour of time. This will allow you time for any technology and table setup, if you are using your own equipment, as well as time to recruit passersby and time to conduct more than one testing session. If you are conducting testing in the field, you will also need to consider additional travel time and work it into your schedule.

If doing formal recruitment, try to include a variety of time slot options for your participants. It works well to give each volunteer participant a list of available times and let him or her select the most convenient ones. Using a free online tool such as Doodle can work well for this, allowing participants to provide their availability across several time slots. You may want to block off an hour of time for scheduled usability tests conducted either in the lab or remotely. This tends to be a standard expectation for research volunteers, and it will allow you to cover a good number of scenarios with each participant. It also might give you some buffer time if you end up having any technical problems. However, as mentioned in chapter 2, you can be flexible with this length of time and can schedule shorter tests, lasting just 15 or 30 minutes long. This may depend on your audience members, their willingness to participate, and the level of incentive you are able to offer them in return for their time.

⌾ Identify a Location

For Intercept Testing

You need to select a good location to successfully conduct intercept testing. In some cases, you might solicit volunteer participants and then walk them to a nearby room for the test. This room would be your version of a usability lab, comparable to what you would use for scheduled sessions. More likely, though, you will be away from this type of controlled environment and will be conducting the testing in a more ad hoc way. In this case, there are a number of other things to consider as you select a location.

You will probably want to go to a high-traffic area where your audience gathers. The first, and easiest, option might be right there in your library building. Your primary audience might be available in your library lobby, computer lab, or exhibit area. If you are targeting participants who are library users, this can be an excellent option. You can set up a table with a laptop or reserve a computer workstation within your computer lab.

If you would rather leave the library building and go out in the field, perhaps recruiting non–library users, you might look at nearby locations that get a lot of foot traffic. If you are looking to recruit members of the general public, perhaps parks, transit centers,

When going out in the field, consider

- Availability of your audience
- Amount of distractions
- Available furniture (tables, chairs)
- Reliability of the Wi-Fi

or shopping malls are locations to consider. If you are on a campus, perhaps student study halls, residence halls, tutoring centers, faculty lounges, or student unions are good options for this type of testing.

At the same time, you will want to try and minimize distractions, if and when possible. You need your participants to be able to focus on the usability test, and you need to be able to both facilitate the test and capture the results with ease. A noisy environment can make this challenging, so you need to try and find a balance between a place with lots of people for recruitment and a place that allows for some quiet focus for conducting the test itself.

Additionally, consider the logistics of the space, including what furniture and technology is available. If you are out in the field using a laptop, you will need to find somewhere that has tables available to work on. You might also want chairs for the facilitator, note taker, and participant. If you are using a tablet or smartphone, this might not be necessary. If you are testing a live version of your website, you will need reliable Wi-Fi at the chosen location.

For Formal Recruitment

When scheduling usability testing in advance, you will also need to identify and secure an appropriate location. In a more formal setting, you may have a usability lab that is dedicated to this purpose, having the required technology and furniture setup for any time you schedule a session. You may have a waiting area outside for participants, especially if you plan to conduct a number of sessions in a row. You may also have a nearby observation room for stakeholders to watch the live session.

This type of a setup can be nice and might be something to aim toward as you plan for ongoing usability testing. In many libraries, though, this won't be feasible given resource and space constraints. Fortunately, a formal usability testing lab certainly isn't a requirement. If you work in a mid-size library, you might have a meeting room or office that can act as a usability lab. You want it to be somewhat quiet, without distractions, and you want to be able to fit the technology and people in the room comfortably.

As you consider your own situation, keep in mind these factors as you select a location for scheduled usability testing sessions:

- You will want to minimize distractions. A quiet room with a door you can keep closed can help with this. Also consider activity happening in rooms next door. For example, don't schedule a usability testing session if a large group is watching a webinar in the next room and the sound might come through the walls.

- If you are using software, you will need a computer that has the software installed. You might just have a single license to the software, in which case you might want it installed on a laptop that is more portable.
- You will likely need a reliable Internet connection. A wired connection might be preferable over Wi-Fi, but if you are using a laptop you may want to check the reliability of the Wi-Fi in the chosen location.
- If participants are meeting you, you will want a location that is easy for them to find. You may consider putting signage in your library lobby directing people where to go.

As you begin usability testing, you might discover that your space needs are different that you originally imagined. You might have some logistical or technical issues with your original location, in which case you will need to be flexible and find an alternative that meets your needs.

Identify Technology to Test On

You will also need to decide what technology you want to test on, assuming you have access to a range of options. Usability testing is often done on a desktop, especially more formal, scheduled usability testing. Yet, with the rise in the variety of devices being used to access websites, and the flexibility allowed by laptop and mobile devices, you ought to consider the various alternatives.

The type of machine and technology being used can contribute to the usability of your website and the level of success a user will have in attempting to complete tasks. Be cautious of assuming that your device, operating system, and browser of choice are in line with those of your audience. Take some time to question your assumptions and experiment using different technology for testing. To start out, you may want to check your web analytics to find out what technology is used most often by your primary audience. Web analytics can tell you which operating systems, browsers, and screen resolutions are being used most often to access your website. You want to first test that your website works well on the technology used most often, and then expand to conduct usability tests on many types of devices over time.

In many cases, you will want to use technology that best matches the technology used by your primary audience. Yet, you may have specific goals for testing that relate to the technology used. For instance, you might have a new responsive design you would like to test with touch-screen and handheld devices. Further, you might be planning on a testing method that would logistically benefit from the flexibility of a handheld device or a tablet.

Additionally, you might have technical requirements to consider. For example, you might plan to conduct usability testing on your staging or development website rather than the website in production. In this case, you will have to ensure you choose technology that can access your development website. In another instance, you might be testing a product that required a Flash Player or the latest version of Java.

So based on your audience behavior, your usability testing goals, your method of testing, and any technical requirements, you can decide what technology is right for your situation. At minimum, technology decisions you will need to make include type of machine, operating system, and browser. The only time this will not be a consideration is, of course, when you are using the participants' technology rather than your own.

© Identify Any Observing or Recording Technology or Facilities

It can be beneficial to have stakeholders observe usability tests. This helps get buy-in on decisions and contributes to a culture of user experience. In commercial environments, it is common to have an observation room where staff members observe usability tests live as they are happening. For this type of setup, you will need technology that presents the usability test to another computer. Usability testing software allows for this, but you can also use webinar software that includes a screen-sharing feature, such as Adobe Connect, WebEx, or Blackboard Collaborate. You can also use Google Hangouts or Skype to share your screen and audio, which allows you to replicate the observation room experience cheaply or completely free.

It is also helpful to record usability tests, allowing you to both review them later during your analysis and share them more broadly with stakeholders. To record the test, you might use usability testing software such as Morae or Silverback. Alternatively, you can use free or low-cost screen recording software. Various software options were covered in chapter 2. Consider your goals when you select software. Cheaper options, such as a webcam alone, might not allow for screen capturing or annotations, so they might be less helpful if you want to share clips with stakeholders, but might be just fine for just-in-case review purposes. As with many of the planning steps, consider your usability testing goals as well as your available resources.

If you do plan to record participants, you may need to have them sign media release forms in order to share the recording later on. Check with your administrators or legal counsel to find out what type of release form might be required, so that you can print them and have them available during the usability testing sessions. Again, this might vary depending on what you intend to do with the recording afterward. Internal use may not require formal consent by the participants, but if you would like to share the recording more broadly, a release form is probably a necessity.

© Obtain Incentives and Recruit Participants

In chapter 2 and table 2.1, a few examples of low-cost incentives were described. You will need to figure out what kind of funding is available for obtaining incentives at your particular organization. You may have an assessment fund, user experience fund, or website fund. Or perhaps you could obtain funding from a donor or from your Friends of the Library. Consider how you might obtain incentives in an ongoing way, perhaps building it into your annual budget. In addition to guiding the type of testing you will be able to conduct and how often, this can be a way to keep up the momentum in your organization.

Incentives and Setup for Recruiting in Person

For intercept testing, recruitment is done on the spot. If you are only anticipating a usability test to last 15 minutes or less, minimal incentives such as drinks and snacks are usually sufficient. Keep in mind that if this is your incentive, it is helpful to include healthy options. Candy bars will work well for some audiences, but having fresh fruit, trail mix, or cereal bars as an alternative may help in recruitment. You can also provide coffee, tea, bottled water, or juice. Other good incentives for intercept recruitment include raffle tickets, T-shirts, tote bags, and coffee mugs.

If you have a set location, you will probably want to set up a table with a tablecloth, your computer for testing, and three chairs: one for the facilitator, one for the participant, and one for the note taker. Keep in mind that if you will be conducting testing for more than an hour, you may need access to a power outlet to keep your computer charged.

For a set location, you should create an easy-to-read sign to help with recruitment. This can be placed prominently on a flip chart or easel near your table. The sign should explain

- What you are doing
- Who you would like to participate
- What the incentive is

For example, the sign could read, "Students: Give us five minutes of your time, help us improve the library website, and get a free candy bar!"

You also want to look official, so make sure that both the facilitator and note taker are wearing name tags. You might even want to wear an official library shirt, if you have one available, so that passersby will notice immediately that you work for the library.

Recruiting Participants in Person

In some cases, you will find that by merely being visible and having a well-written sign, you will have passersby stop and volunteer to participate. There will be little need to approach people, as they will come to you. In other cases, you will need to be proactive in order to get volunteers to participate. To do this, simply approach people and ask them if they have a few minutes to help you improve the library website.

As you begin talking to potential participants, be welcoming, friendly, and willing to answer any questions they might have. Try to avoid coming off as pushy or aggressive in any way. You are more likely to receive a positive response if you are casual and approachable than if you are insistent or forceful. If your potential participants seem hesitant at first, be sure to let them know that

- It is for a good cause: "to help improve the library website"
- It won't take much time: "no more than 10 minutes"

Be aware that you will often have people turn you down, and this is to be expected. Sometimes, you might be able to encourage them to come by later or even gather their contact information to schedule a usability test at a time that is more convenient for them.

Be thoughtful about who you approach, and avoid approaching those who are clearly busy with other things. You don't want to bother people who are in a rush to get some-

TIP FOR INTERCEPT RECRUITMENT: BE VISIBLE

Having some visible incentives can help get the notice of potential participants. If you are out in the field, try holding a basket full of treats while you are walking around. If you have a table set up, use a tablecloth and have T-shirts, pens, and coffee mugs presented nicely for passersby to see.

where, on are on the phone, reading or studying, or having an intimate conversation with somebody next to them. Be careful to not interrupt or disrupt people if they are in the middle of something. People who are doing more leisurely activities, such as surfing the web, eating a snack, or strolling by, will be more likely to give you a few minutes of their time than people who are anxiously trying to finish up some important work.

Recruiting Your Target Audience in Person

You may be hoping to recruit participants who will have similar behavior to your audience, perhaps having a certain level of technical, domain, or functional knowledge. You can plan for this by writing out some inclusion and exclusion criteria. This is similar to what is done for clinical trials in order to control the study and get valid results. For example, you might be conducting a usability test of a room reservation system from a smartphone. An inclusion criterion might be a level of comfort using touch-screen, handheld devices. In order to get authentic results, you want all participants to have this characteristic. An exclusion criterion might be experience reserving a room using this system. If a volunteer has already used the system, you want to exclude him or her from participating, since he or she will bring previous knowledge and experience and will likely behave differently because of this.

When you are recruiting passersby, there are two methods that can help with this. First, be sure that your sign lets people know what sort of volunteers you need in a broad sense. Perhaps your sign reads, "Graduate students needed!" or "Are you a parent of a teenager?" This way, people will know who you are looking for and will probably only volunteer if they fall within that category. Second, you can prepare a set of more specific questions based around your inclusion and exclusion criteria. You will then simply ask your volunteers these questions before beginning the test. In the room reservation example, questions would be something like

- Do you own a smartphone?
- Have you booked a library room before?

If you are only interested in a particular audience and feel that it would not be helpful to conduct usability testing with people who fall outside of this audience, you can then include or exclude the volunteer based on his or her answers to these questions. Alternatively, you can proceed with the usability test, just taking this information into account during the analysis phase. If you do exclude the person, you may want to provide the incentive anyway, to thank him or her for stopping by.

Asking volunteers these questions is usually a better approach than trying to make initial judgment calls on passersby, guessing at who might fit within your audience. You want to avoid unfairly profiling somebody based on appearance. A better tactic is to approach people nondiscriminatory and then simply ask them a question or two to ensure they are a member of your audience.

Inclusion criteria: characteristics that participants must have to participate in the study

Exclusion criteria: characteristics that will exclude participants from the study

TIPS ON APPROACHING STRANGERS

Recruiting volunteers in person can often be the most challenging part of intercept usability testing. You may not enjoy feeling like a solicitor and may feel as if you are bothering or annoying people. Many people are not comfortable approaching strangers and asking for their help, and take things personally if they have people ignoring them or turning them down. It is something that gets better with practice and becomes easier over time, but can remain challenging.

As you approach strangers, keep in mind that you will get people who turn you down and that it's completely normal. Some people are busy, are not interested, or are having a bad day. They might say, "No," or they might completely ignore you. You may have people be rude to you. This is normal and not something to take personally. It is something to be expected when you are approaching strangers.

Some people are better at soliciting volunteer passersby than others. You might find that student workers are more comfortable approaching other students, and more extroverted librarians are more comfortable than introverted ones. It is something worth considering as far as staffing the activity and selecting a method of testing. It might be that a library volunteer or student worker would be a more appropriate person to play the role of recruiter for intercept tests, or it might be that scheduling sessions in advance is a better option for you.

Recruiting Participants in Advance

For usability testing appointments scheduled in advance, you are able to do more targeted recruitment. After reading chapter 4 and considering your audience behavior as it relates to the tasks you plan to test, you should have an idea of what type of targeted recruitment efforts will be necessary. Table 5.3 shows examples of tasks, their target audience, and ideas for recruitment. In some cases, if you are recruiting a broad audience, flyers placed in high-traffic areas and messages on Facebook, Twitter, and the library website are good approaches. In other cases where you are interested in a smaller segment of your audience, individual invitations by librarians can be your best option.

When you are formally recruiting participants, gift cards and raffles for larger prizes are good options for incentives. In addition to offering an explicit incentive, your promotional material should also say that their participation will improve the library website or service. In general, you may find good will from current or prospective users toward the library. As educational or nonprofit institutions, libraries often receive a positive response from users when they ask for this type of assistance.

Recruiting Your Target Audience in Advance

You will also need to decide whether to share with the volunteers any inclusion and exclusion criteria in your recruitment materials, or whether you would like to handle this on a case-by-case basis. If you include this information in the recruitment efforts, it will save you the time of asking volunteers these questions later on. Do you only want instructors from a particular department? Do you only want a certain age range? Do you only want

Table 5.3. Example of Recruitment Efforts Based on Tasks and Target Audience

TASKS	AUDIENCE	RECRUITMENT TYPE
• Create a customized resource guide for a class • Request a suite of tutorials be embedded in the course management system	English composition instructors	• English composition e-mail list • Department newsletter • Personal, individual invitations by e-mail and phone
• Request a long-term study room • Apply for a dissertation writing room • Reserve a comprehensive exam room	Graduate students working toward their PhD	• Flyers in graduate student lounge • Flyers in graduate lockers • Department e-mail lists • Graduate and Professional Student Council e-mail list • Library Facebook page • Library Twitter account

people who have never used your library website, or never used a particular service you are testing? Recruitment in advance allows you to be more targeted in this way, inviting only volunteers who fit within a very particular segment of your audience.

At the same time, you might exclude a significant number of participants by requiring too specific of a set of characteristics, when the results could still be helpful even if not all participants meet all the characteristics perfectly. You may start out being quite strict with your criteria, but be aware you may need to become more flexible if it turns out that you are having a hard time recruiting the number of people you would like.

Recruiting in General

No matter the type of recruitment you are using, whether it is in person or in advance, you want to make sure to include the following information:

EXAMPLE RECRUITMENT E-MAIL

Dear Professor Irwin,

The library is working hard to improve our website. We are currently inviting faculty from the history department to participate in a research activity where we will ask you to complete a few tasks on the website and tell us how it goes. It will take no longer than an hour. This information will be extremely valuable to us, and will help us make some positive changes to the website. To thank you for your time, you will be entered in a raffle to win a Kindle Fire.

Please let us know if you are available any time between 8 a.m. and 5 p.m. on these days: Tuesday, December 3rd; Friday, December 6th; Monday, December 9th.

Let me know if you have any questions, and feel free to share this invitation with any colleagues who might also be interested!

Best,
Rebecca

- It will help improve the website.
- It will take no more than X (amount of time).
- You will receive X (incentive) to thank you for your time.

There is additional content you will want to include depending on your method of testing. For instance, if you are planning to use the participants' technology, you will want to let them know that they will be required to have a particular level of technology with them. If you are conducting the testing remotely using a screen-capturing software, you will want to let them know this, as well. Essentially, you just want to be sure to include the relevant information that will help the participants decide whether they would like to volunteer.

Other Logistics

A number of other logistics might be worth thinking about during the planning phase. These will vary greatly depending upon your method of testing.

To lend your effort some credibility, you may want to ask your marketing department or a graphic artist on staff to help create the recruitment materials. This could include mass e-mails, social media postings, or flyers around the building, as well as a sign for the day of testing.

If you are conducting intercept testing in a set location, you might need to secure a table, tablecloth, and chairs. You might also want to find a flip chart or easel to display your recruitment sign, and may want to display your incentives in a large basket or in gift bags.

For testing out in the field, it is helpful to wear an official name tag so that potential participants can tell that you are library staff members. You also will want to appear approachable, so you might consider wearing more casual clothing on the day of the testing. If you are traveling a distance or testing for a few hours at a time, you will want to be wearing comfortable shoes as well.

You might want to print out copies of the scenarios to give to the participants. The note taker might want to secure a clipboard, paper, and pen, or may consider taking notes on a tablet or other portable device.

Depending upon your chosen location, you might need to ask for permission to be there. In a public space in your library building, you may have to consult with facilities or public services staff members to confirm they are OK with it. In a public location, you may need to check to make sure permission isn't required beforehand if you plan to solicit

DO I NEED IRB APPROVAL?

If you work in a university setting, you may need to find out if Institutional Review Board (IRB) approval is required for the method of usability testing you plan to conduct. If it is required, this will add an additional step to your planning process.

In many cases, IRB approval will not be necessary. At the University of Arizona, IRB approval is only required when the intention is to generalize the results to a broad population. Since the results are used primarily to improve a particular website, IRB approval is not required for the vast majority of usability testing conducted.

CHECKLIST FOR PLANNING A USABILITY TEST

❑ Identify a facilitator and note taker
❑ Write tasks and define success
❑ Translate tasks into scenarios
❑ Test your scenarios (read them out loud, share them with someone)
❑ Secure your incentives
❑ Select a time and location
❑ Secure a computer and any software you need
❑ Recruit participants in advance or have a plan for intercept recruitment

passersby. When appropriate, you might want to let people know beforehand where you plan to conduct usability testing so that they are aware of it.

Key Points

Planning for a usability test has a number of components. Essentially, you need to figure out who is going to do it, what they are going to do, and how they are going to do it. Remember:

- You need to clearly define your tasks and understand what success will look like.
- Your scenarios need to be concise, specific, and non-leading.
- You should choose a time, location, and technology that will help you recruit participants, facilitate the test effectively, and reach your testing goals.
- You should select incentives and recruitment methods that make sense given your audience and your method of testing.

With scenarios written down, logistics taken care of, and the planning phase complete, it is now time to actually conduct a usability test.

Conducting a Usability Test

WITH ALL PLANNING STEPS COMPLETED, it is time to conduct the usability test. The key elements to conducting the test are the facilitation and the note taking. The facilitator needs to know how to introduce, facilitate, and end the test. The note taker needs to know how to capture what is most important, and how to identify success and failure to complete tasks.

Welcome Participants and Make Introductions

Once your participants arrive, you will want to introduce yourself and your note taker, if you have one. You want your participants to feel comfortable and relaxed, because it is important that they feel they can talk with you and express themselves honestly. So try to be calm, welcoming, and approachable. Introduce yourself, smile, and thank them for being there.

It is likely that you, as facilitator, have a close connection with the website you are about to test. This isn't ideal, since the facilitator needs to be objective, but you need to work with what you have available. If participants are aware that you built or designed the website, though, this might make them hesitant to provide honest, candid feedback on any problems they experience. For this reason, you might want to avoid sharing the details of your role when it comes to the website. Rather, just say that you work at the library or that you are working on the web project.

You will also want to briefly explain what the role of the facilitator and the note taker will be during the session. The facilitator will be moderating the activity and answering any questions. The note taker will be observing and capturing notes.

Get Permissions and Introduce the Technology

If you are recording the usability session, you may need to ask participants to sign a consent form. This is something you will need to ask them to do at the very start of the session, before the initial interview, if you plan to record it. If you are only planning to record the actual usability test, you can ask for their signature after the initial interview but before introducing the test.

It may make sense to talk about permission releases at the same time you talk about what technology you are using for the recording. It might be that you need to press buttons on the computer during the session to track start and stop points for the scenarios, or do some other sort of technical modifications along the way. Introducing this now will make this interruption not come as a surprise to the participants during the test and will avoid a potentially awkward distraction during the session.

Also, if you have observers watching remotely, you ought to tell the participants at this time. You don't want to make the participants nervous, but you do want to be honest with them about the extent of observation and recording that will take place.

If you are conducting a remote usability test, this would also be the time to check any technology. You will want to make sure your screen-sharing and/or screen-capturing tools are working correctly, and that any audio or video is being transmitted clearly.

Conduct the Initial Interview

Once everyone is introduced and settled in place, the facilitator should complete a brief interview with the participant. The purpose of this interview is to gather any background information about him or her that will help you in both conducting an effective test and analyzing the results from the test. It is also a way to get the participant comfortable talking with you.

During the planning phase, you considered factors that might influence a participant's behavior when it comes to your website. The screening questions from chapter 5 allowed you to include or exclude participants from your study in the initial recruitment phase. Similar types of questions can be asked during the initial interview. These questions aren't to exclude anyone from your study, but they will provide you with data that will be helpful during the usability test itself as well as the analysis phase. Examples of the types of questions to include are in table 6.1.

Table 6.1. Example of Initial Interview Questions

TO FIND OUT	ASK
Participants' comfort level with technology	How often do you use the Internet? How often do you use a tablet? Do you own a smartphone?
Their familiarity with the library website	Have you used this website before, and how often? What have you used it for?
Their familiarity with your library or similar libraries	How often do you use this library? Have you used other libraries?
Their familiarity with a particular resource or service, or a similar resource or service	Have you used this particular library service before? Have you used similar services offered by other libraries or organizations?
Their expectations of or assumptions about the library	Have you had a negative or positive experience with your library or website, or with a similar organization?

Introduce the Test

Once you have completed the initial interview, you can move on to introducing the usability test itself. At this point, participants may or may not know what the usability test is all about. Either way, it is good practice to explain the purpose of the test and how long it will take. In the introduction, be sure to mention the following to the participants:

- It will take X amount of time.
- The purpose is to improve the website.
- You cannot do anything wrong.
- You should speak out loud as much as possible (assuming you are using the "thinking aloud" technique, discussed later).
- You should be honest and nothing you say will hurt our feelings.
- We will give you a scenario and then ask you to try to find (or do) something on the website.
- Tell us when you think you have completed the scenario.
- Here is how the technology will work (if needed).
- You must follow these rules (if there are any).

Length of Time

Be sure to tell participants how long the session will take. For more informal tests, you might have to make an educated guess, given the tasks you plan to test. One approach is to tell them the maximum amount of time you expect it to take. For instance, you can say, "This will take no more than 10 minutes of your time." If that is the case, be sure to stick to that promise. Alternatively, you can say an approximate length of time, as vague as "only a few minutes of your time" or more specific, "about 30 minutes of your time."

For scheduled tests, you have probably scheduled a specific length of time. During the introduction, you would just remind participants of this and let them know it may take less time than that, but it is a matter of going through the scenarios and seeing how long it takes.

What is interesting about approximating time is that the length of time it takes to go through the scenarios may vary greatly depending on the participant. What takes one participant 10 minutes to complete may take another 30 minutes to complete. Because of this expected variation, it helps to be flexible with both the time and the number of scenarios you plan to go through.

The Purpose

As you likely expressed in your recruitment materials, the purpose of the usability test is to improve your website. This is something to convey again during the introduction of the test. When participants are fully aware that this is the purpose, they are more likely to be honest and more likely to spend the time giving you helpful information.

Testing the Website, Not the Participant

The participants must understand that they cannot do anything wrong. Express to the participants that you are testing the website; you are not testing them. For this reason, they cannot do anything wrong. Similarly, let the participants know that they cannot hurt your feelings. Their honest reactions to things are what will be the most helpful.

Speaking Out Loud

Essential to a useful usability test is for the participants to express their thoughts out loud. This will help you understand why they are clicking on the links or buttons they are clicking on, what content they are reading (or not reading), what terminology they use, and how confident they are as they are making a decision. In the introduction, you should ask the participants to talk out loud as much as possible when they go through the scenarios, sharing information about what they are looking at, what they are doing, and what they are thinking and feeling.

Described by Rubin and Chisnell (2008, 204–206) as the "thinking aloud" technique, this is the most common approach. There is an alternative to this for special cases, which will be discussed in the facilitation section.

How It Will Work

Naturally, you will want to tell participants what to expect. You should tell them that you will be reading through a number of scenarios that will direct them to complete tasks on your website. You can mention if you have printed copies of the scenarios for them, and you may also want to tell them the number of scenarios so they have a sense of what to expect to cover in the allotted amount of time. Also be sure to let them know that they can ask questions at any time. While you won't be able to guide them or help them in actually completing the tasks, you will be able to clarify any confusion they have related to the process.

Rules to Give the Participant

Depending on the goals of your usability test, you may want to give participants certain rules to follow as they are attempting to complete tasks. A common rule is to stay on

COMMON RULES

- Stay on this website.
- Do not use the site search.
- Do not use Ask a Librarian.

the website that is being tested. Going out to other websites, such as your main campus website or a related website, or to search engines such as Google might not give you the information you need to improve your website. However, if you are interested in the broader user journey and want to see how users would actually go about completing a task in real life, you may want to leave this open as an option to them.

Another common rule is to not use the website search feature. If you are trying to find out if your navigation is useful, allowing participants to use the site search will not give you that information. Again, though, you may not want this rule if you are trying to keep the test as authentic as possible and actually see how people would go about using your website with no rules in place. In libraries, there are often numerous search options, and this can be a cause of confusion for participants. If you create a rule about not using a search feature, be sure that you are very clear on what you mean by this. For instance, if you tell the participants they aren't able to use the site search, is this referring to the search box in the center of the home page, the search box in the upper right corner, a magnifying glass icon that represents search, a menu drop-down titled "Search," or a link that includes the word *search*? This has been a cause of confusion in usability tests in libraries, so be thoughtful about how you frame a rule having to do with search. Be as clear and concise as possible, and let them know you can clarify this if needed.

EXAMPLE INTRODUCTORY SCRIPT

The following script is adapted from Krug (2010, 70–71):

> We appreciate you taking the time to help us today. We are working to improve our library website and are asking people to try completing a few tasks so that we can see how things are working (or not) and make things work a bit better. This should take no longer than 15 minutes of your time. There is no right or wrong way to do things, and you cannot make any mistakes. We are testing the website; we aren't testing you.
>
> We'd like you to speak out loud as much as possible. Tell us what you are looking at, what you are trying to do, and what you are thinking. This will really help us. Please be honest and don't worry about hurting our feelings. We need to hear your honest reactions so we can improve the website.
>
> You can ask clarification questions along the way, but be aware that I might not be able to answer them, mostly because I can't tell you how to do something on the website, because the purpose is to see what you would do if no one was here to help you. The only rules are that you can't use the site search feature, and you need to stay on this website.
>
> Do you have any questions before we begin?

Further, there may be other types of rules depending on what you make available on your website. For instance, you may have an Ask a Librarian feature that provides live chat help. If this is the case, you may make a rule that participants cannot use Ask a Librarian to find the answer to their question. Perhaps you also don't want them to use a frequently asked questions page or a help page; you want to see if they can find the information where it lives on the website.

Again, consider the goals of your test and what you are trying to find out. You may start out with no rules as an experiment to see what information you discover, then add rules as needed later on.

Begin with a Tour of the Home Page

In traditional usability tests, you begin by asking participants about their general impressions of your website, asking them a few open-ended questions about the home page before reading any of the scenarios. This might be useful to include in your usability tests, depending on your goals and the time you have allotted. A tour of the home page would be useful to include if you are interested in the general perception of your organization, what it does, and how it can help them. By asking for these overall impressions, you may discover some concerns with particular design elements such as fonts, colors, and images, as well as any usability problems such as readability and global navigation issues. You might hear feedback that there is too much content or there are too many links on the home page, making it difficult to know where to start. You also can gain insight into what participants think they can accomplish on the website, which can be helpful to evaluate the design focus and to what extent the website reflects the primary tasks of its users.

To facilitate a home page tour, first bring up your website in a browser. Direct the participants not to actually click on anything, but that it is OK to scroll and look around. The purpose of this is to get their initial impressions of the home page. This usually works best for participants who have not used your website before. Then ask them such questions as

- What do you notice about this website? What stands out to you?
- What do you think you can do here?
- What kind of information do you think you could find here?
- What are your overall impressions of this website on first glance?

The general comments that you receive at this stage can be helpful to share with stakeholders. If the comments are positive, you can demonstrate that the home page is viewed favorably by users. If they are negative, you can justify the need to make some changes to the home page or overall theme of the website.

Facilitate Effectively

After the home page tour, it is time to read your first scenario. If you are providing participants with a printed copy, you will want to first read it out loud, and then hand it to them as a reference. You may ask participants to read the scenario out loud themselves and ask any clarification questions they have about the scenario prior to attempting to complete it. Once the scenario is read and the participants are ready to go, your role is now to facilitate the activity.

Keep Them Talking (Usually)

To get the most useful results from usability tests, your participants need to explain what they are doing and why they are doing it. A usability test without the context of *why* a participant did what he or she did can be pretty meaningless, and analysis becomes much harder. This is one of the reasons why unmoderated remote testing can be very challenging.

You might get a sense of what participants are thinking by their body language and expressions, but it really helps if they are able to verbalize their thought process. Sometimes called the think-aloud or talk-aloud protocol, this is usually your best option for gathering your participants' thoughts: at the moment they are having them.

You have already asked participants to speak out loud when you introduced the test. The effort required by you, as facilitator, will very much depend on the individual participant's personality and comfort level in sharing his or her thoughts out loud. In some cases, there may be very little need for you to jump in at all. Most likely, though, you will have to interject the occasional probing or clarifying question to keep participants speaking out loud.

It is a balance. While you want to hear their thoughts, you need to be careful not to interrupt them any more than necessary. You want to avoid interfering with participants' natural thought processes and progressions as they attempt to complete the tasks. You don't want to distract them from what they are doing or cause them to lose their train of thought. In an authentic environment, users won't be distracted with questions as they are trying to complete tasks on your website. So in addition to causing them distraction, your questions may also influence their behavior with your website and alter your test results.

It is OK and expected to have moments of silence here or there. Be patient, trying not to break participants' concentration unnecessarily. When the participant is at a stopping point and you aren't clear on what he or she is thinking, that is a good time to ask a brief probing question to get him or her talking again. Be thoughtful and intentional about when to interject, and use your words carefully. Here are some good general probing questions to use:

- What are you thinking?
- What are you looking for?
- What are you doing now?
- Do you feel like you are getting closer?

In some cases, there might be a good reason to not have participants speak out loud during the actual activity. Perhaps you are trying to capture "time on task," which is the amount of time it takes to complete a particular task. Since talking out loud will slow participants down, you may want to avoid this. Or perhaps your target audience segment would have difficulty verbalizing their thoughts at the same time as working with the computer, due to their lower level of technical knowledge. Another case might be that the type of thing being tested simply doesn't lend itself well to a talk-aloud approach. Perhaps you are asking participants to go through a tutorial, step-by-step, where the main interaction is just their reading content on the screen and trying to process the content before moving forward. You don't want them to be distracted by trying to talk out loud as they are reading, and they aren't making decisions along the way or performing tasks in the traditional sense.

If you are in any of these types of situations, you can avoid the talk-aloud protocol and alternatively conduct a "retrospective review" in which you replay the recorded test after the fact and ask participants to discuss their thought process in hindsight (Rubin and Chisnell 2008). You can also do a hybrid version where you ask them to talk out loud during the test, but don't ever probe them or ask clarifying questions so as to not distract them. You can simply ask them to reflect upon their experience afterward and ask any questions you have at that time.

Ask Clarifying Questions

Since you want to know *why* participants are doing what they are doing, you may find it helpful to ask clarifying questions during the test, as well. These are questions to make sure you understand what participants are feeling or what they are telling you. Again, though, be careful not to distract participants unnecessarily. Only ask questions if you think it is important information that will help you during the analysis phase. A good time to ask a clarifying question is when the participant

- Makes an interesting facial expression (i.e., rolling eyes, biting lower lip, raising eyebrow)
- Makes an unexpected selection without describing why
- Describes something but not clearly enough that you understand it
- Acts surprised or confused by what just happened
- Selects the back button, but doesn't say why

Some useful clarification questions are

- Can you tell me what you are thinking right now?
- Can you tell me why you selected that?
- Do you mean the X over there?
- Is that what you intended to select?
- Is that what you expected to happen?
- Is that what you expected to see on this page?

WHEN TO SAVE QUESTIONS FOR LATER

You might find that a particular participant is difficult to "read," and you feel a need to ask a lot of probing and clarifying questions. If this is the case, it can be worthwhile to hold off on asking all of the questions right away.

Again, you want to avoid distracting participant too much as they go through this process. If you are asking too many questions, this can become burdensome and can extend the length of the test. Simply jot down questions you have, or keep them in mind, and ask them at the end of the test, once all of the tasks are completed.

Be sure to keep your questions neutral. The same way that there is no right or wrong way to approach a task, there should be no right or wrong way to answer the facilitator's probing or clarifying questions.

Manage Their Emotions

Participants will frequently get frustrated when they are unable to complete a task easily. Oftentimes, participants will think that they are doing something wrong, even though you have told them that they can't do anything wrong.

One of the keys to effective facilitating is handling these moments of frustration and keeping the test going. In fact, these moments can be the most helpful, as they often demonstrate a significant usability problem that you weren't previously aware of. Hopefully, such participants are still willing to try and haven't given up just yet. If this is the case, encourage them to keep going, to try something different, and to talk more about what they expected to see or expected to happen and where things seemed to go wrong.

Make sure that frustrated participants know that they are providing you with helpful information. Be empathetic and keep the focus on the website, not on the participant. Say things to let them know that you understand their frustration and that they are providing you with helpful information, for example,

- "I can see you are getting frustrated, but this is an important part of the website we need to improve. Do you mind trying for just a couple more minutes?"
- "This is turning out to be a tough scenario. I appreciate your patience as you deal with our website! We will clearly have to make some changes."
- "I know this is difficult, but this is really helpful for us. We will definitely use this information to make some improvements to our website."

Throughout your interactions with participants, be careful to avoid getting frustrated yourself. Keep a cool, calm demeanor, and remind yourself (and the participants) that this is just an activity to help improve the website.

Remain Neutral

As facilitator, you need to remain impartial throughout the session. Avoid expressing your opinions or emotions, and never give participants advice on what to do or not do.

A participant might take the expected path and seamlessly complete the assigned task. While it can be tempting, don't tell the participant that it was the correct path or the correct answer. You can say, "Great," and move on, but don't say, "That's right, good job!" Even though this is a nice thing to say and it will make the participant feel good, it implies that there is a right and a wrong way to do things, which there is not.

Conversely, you may discover that a participant completes a task taking a different route than you would have expected. Avoid saying anything such as, "Oh, interesting!" or "Well, that's not what you were supposed to do." Even without saying anything, be careful of your nonverbal reactions to things. Avoid sighing or saying, "Hmm," as it might have implications to the study. It is important that you not demonstrate any level of approval or disapproval of the participant's actions.

It cannot be stressed enough that you should never express to participants that they did something incorrectly. As you said in the introduction, participants cannot do anything wrong. Be sure to stick to that in your interactions with them during the test itself. Also, be cautious of your body language and facial expressions. You may be frustrated, confused, or even annoyed about what you are observing, but stay calm and collected for the purposes of the test. Providing the participants with any indication that you yourself are frustrated will only agitate the situation and negatively affect the experience.

Don't Guide

You also need to be careful not to guide participants in any way. The purpose of a usability test is to see how real users would try to complete a task without anybody's help. You can clarify the scenario if participants are unclear on what they are supposed to try to do, but that is the extent of the help you should be providing.

You may find that a participant directly asks you for help, perhaps saying, "Should I click on the X over there?" Similarly, the participant might ask for confirmation that he or she is doing the "right" thing, such as, "Is that where I was supposed to go?" or "Am I on the right track?" When a participant asks you something like this, respond by saying something like, "What do you think?" or "What would you do next if you were trying to do this from home?" Again, as you expressed in the introduction, you may want to remind the participant that you need to see what he or she would do if no one was there to help. You can reiterate that this will be much more helpful than if you explain what to do.

It can be hard to not help participants when they are struggling, especially for people within the library profession where helping patrons is a primary job responsibility. When providing information and assistance is your job, it can actually feel quite uncomfortable at first to stay quiet when you really want to guide participants in the "right" direction.

Listen to Their Suggestions, but Don't Take Them Too Seriously

Oftentimes, participants will want to give you advice on how to improve the website. As they struggle to complete tasks or as they eventually complete a task after a few attempts, they might want to share their ideas on how to fix the problem. This is a natural inclination, and you should allow them to express this advice if they want to. Occasionally, you will gain good insight and may even implement a suggestion made by a participant. More often, though, suggestions from participants would not actually be feasible or useful improvements.

Participants have a very limited knowledge of the website's content, architecture, and technical capabilities. They have often only been exposed to a small segment of the website's content, and so have a small slice of the overall perspective on the problem. They also don't tend to have a background in user experience design. So while there is a chance they will come up with a helpful idea for an improvement, it is unlikely.

So when a participant shares a suggestion, capture it within the notes, and respond with something like, "That is worth thinking about," or "That is an option we'll consider." Be sure not to imply that you will implement their suggestions, just that it is one option that you will have to discuss after you have gathered more data.

It is the job of the participants to make you aware of how actual users interact with your website. They can let you know where your website fails, but they can rarely advise you on practical solutions for fixing those problems.

Use Good Judgment

This is a human process, and every usability test is going to be a bit different. Participants are actual people with different personalities, abilities, temperaments, and levels of patience. A good facilitator has good judgment on when to chime in and when to keep silent, as well as how to keep the participant from getting too frustrated. Remember that you have some knowledge of the participant's background from both the initial screening (if you had one) and the initial interview. Use this information, along with your interpersonal skills, to make the usability test both a useful and pleasant experience. It might be a bit rocky at first, but realize that your judgment will improve as you conduct more usability tests.

Don't Worry Too Much

You are human, and humans make mistakes. It is normal and OK if you break some of the facilitation rules at first. Even usability tests with faulty facilitation will provide you with helpful information about your website. Just pay attention to when you make mistakes so that you can avoid making them the next time. Facilitating usability tests can be a bit uncomfortable and awkward initially. After some practice, though, you will make fewer mistakes and will be able to communicate with participants more naturally, and it will become an easier, more enjoyable process overall.

⑥ Take Useful Notes

Notes will be a great help when you are analyzing your results. Even if you are recording the test in its entirety using usability testing software, you will find it helpful to supplement the recording with some hand-curated notes that highlight the most interesting moments.

WHAT ABOUT TEAM TESTING?

It is possible to conduct team tests where you have two or even three participants work to complete tasks collaboratively. The initial interview may take a bit longer, since you will have to interview each participant. Facilitation is pretty much the same, although you will find that there is less need to probe or ask clarifying questions since the participants will be talking to each other. This is actually a helpful advantage of team testing: there is less need to distract participants with your questions.

Note taking can be trickier, because you might want to capture each individual's actions and comments for more comprehensive analysis. You don't have to do this, though. The main thing you want to capture is still the computer interactions and any useful comments, very much the same as you would with an individual participant. The challenge is that you will probably hear more comments than you would from an individual participant, so you may have to be more selective on which ones to capture.

Notes are usually taken in real time during the observation of the test, but they can also be taken after the fact if you have a full recording of the test. There are many methods of taking good notes, and over time you will find the method that best works for your own context.

The note taker might use a laptop to capture what is going on, or might create handwritten notes. For scheduled testing, the note taker might capture the notes online using a document sharing tool such as Google Drive, actually allowing observers to see the notes as they are being written in real time. This is an interesting technique for allowing real-time observation by stakeholders with minimal technical requirements, and allows observers to make comments or ask questions that the note taker could then relay to the facilitator or ask at the closing of the session.

For more informal, on-the-fly testing, the note taker may just scribe using a pencil and notepad, capturing notes for all tests conducted on a particular day. Once the testing is over, the note taker might clean up what he or she wrote and transcribe it into a Word document that can be shared with the web team.

Depending on the situation and the note taker's abilities, he or she may be able to capture the entirety of what is going on accurately and comprehensively, or the person might have to pick and choose which interactions and comments to capture. More likely, you will find yourself in the second scenario, where the note taker must capture what he or she feels is most important rather than try to capture every single thing.

Capture Participant Information

You will want to capture information about the participant involved in the test. In particular, you will want to capture the participant's responses to the initial interview questions. These will tell you about the participant's background and will be helpful data to consider during the analysis phase. This will also be helpful as you try to recall details of a particular usability testing session. You may not immediately remember the person who clicked on a certain series of links, but you will probably remember the person who was a 35-year-old PhD student and an avid library user.

Capture Tasks, Navigation, Attempts, and Success or Failure

As the participant attempts to complete tasks, the note taker will need to pay attention to how the participant is interacting with the website and capture that interaction as clearly as possible. For each task, you want to capture the navigation path, the number of attempts, and whether the task was completed successfully.

In most cases, you will be asking participants to complete more than one task. The note taker ought to first capture the task name or number as it is read to the participant. Now, the participant will start to interact with the website. Primarily, the note taker should try to capture each instance where the participant interacts with the navigation. Most of these interactions with be clicking or selecting a link, button, menu, tab, or other element. There may also be interactions that don't involve an actual click, but do imply an effort to navigate. When using a mouse, this could be something like hovering over an icon that displays a pop-out window or hovering over a header that displays a drop-down menu. When using a touch screen, this could be something like scrolling horizontally to move an image carousel. By capturing these types of interactions in the notes, you will capture the path that the participant took to attempt to complete a task. In its simplest form, this will be a trail of clicks or links. In a more complicated case, it might be a combination of interactions. A helpful way to capture the participant's navigation path is to use the caret symbol (>) between each click. For example,

Services > Services A–Z > Computer Labs

It is helpful to mark each attempt the participant makes to complete a task. An attempt is defined as when the participant goes down a particular direct path in hopes of completing the task. If the participant clicks the back button or goes to a different navigation item outside of the path he or she was previously on, that is considered another attempt. The reason attempts are important is because they are good indicators of the amount of effort it took the participant to complete the task. When a participant starts a new attempt, you might want to mark where he or she tripped up with a question mark. For example,

- Attempt 1: Services > Services A-Z > Computer Labs — ?
- Attempt 2: Services > Study Spaces & Computing > Software

Ultimately, the participant will either succeed or fail at completing each task. This is something to capture in the notes at the end of the section for that particular task. You may find it helpful to use color coding to make this information stand out, indicating success in green and failure in red.

Use Codes, Abbreviations, and Symbols

Participants can talk quickly and can interact with your website quickly, making it a challenge for the note taker to capture everything. To save the time of the note taker and make sure as much information as possible is transcribed, it is helpful to come up with codes or abbreviations for some common things.

If you have initial interview questions, you will benefit from assigning numbers to these questions rather than writing them out, so that you simply have something like *Q1* to represent the first question. You also might ask yes/no questions or questions with common answers. *Yes* or *No* can become *Y* or *N*. Undergraduate student can be represented by *UG*, graduate student can be represented by *G*, and member of the public can be represented by *P*.

Similarly to the way you would assign numbers to your interview questions, you can assign numbers to each task or scenario. This way, rather than writing out the potentially lengthy scenario as it is read to the participant, the note taker can simply write T1, T2, and so on. Alternatively, you could create short code names for each task, such as *Task: Book*, *Task: Article*, and so on.

It can be a challenge for a note taker to capture everything the participant clicks on while attempting to complete a task, as this can go by very quickly. To help with this, you might want to assign abbreviations to your primary navigation items on your website. As you conduct additional rounds of usability testing, you will find that many navigation items are clicked on over and over again. Rather than asking the note taker to capture the full name of each item clicked on, you can provide him or her with abbreviations for these commonly used ones. For example, *Search and Find* can be abbreviated *S&F*, and *Print, Copy, Scan* can be abbreviated *PSC*. It could be beneficial to create these abbreviations up front, but you could also just advise your note taker to use these sort of obvious abbreviations as they are taking notes, especially if he or she finds that certain links or menu items are clicked on multiple times.

It is helpful to have some standard symbols to capture participants' interaction with the website, as well. As already mentioned, a caret symbol (>) can be used to identify a click or tap. If participants are typing, you may want to use a standard for this, such as [typed: xyz]. When participants scroll down, you could use arrows to indicate a downward, upward, or horizontal scroll.

Consider the tasks you will be testing, your website features and navigation elements, and what interactions are most likely. Over time, you can build up a set of common abbreviations and codes for the note taker, allowing him or her to conduct notes more efficiently.

Create a Template

Creating a template for note taking can be very helpful and can alleviate some of the need for abbreviations. You will find a template most helpful if you are conducting a number of similar tests with the same interview questions and the same tasks.

In a template, you can include a place to capture participants' answers to the interview questions, since the questions will be standard for all participants. If there are common answers to those questions, you could include those answers, allowing the note taker to simply circle the answer rather than having to write it down.

If creating a template, be sure to include plenty of room to capture comments from the participants. These comments can be attached to particular attempts to complete a task and can be overall comments on the particular round

EXAMPLE OF NOTE TAKING TEMPLATE

Interview Questions:

Status: Undergraduate Graduate Faculty Staff Library Staff Other _____

Used website: Yes No Comments _____

Scenario 1: You want to drop off a book that is due tomorrow. What time does the library close today?

Attempt 1:

Attempt 2:

Attempt 3:

Success? Yes No

Comments: _____

Lessons learned: _____

Capture Helpful Comments

Some of the most useful data collected during usability tests are the comments made by participants as they attempt to complete tasks. Only by capturing what the participants say will you capture the full story of any given test. These comments can also be helpful for communicating results to stakeholders, since they tell a more human story than the navigation paths and success rates alone. If you are using software to record the test, you might want to focus on just capturing comments in your notes and associate those comments with particular times in the recording, making it easier to go back and review them or share them with stakeholders.

Capturing all comments can be challenging, since a talkative participant can be difficult to transcribe word for word. For this reason, the note taker ought to focus on capturing those comments that are particularly important or that will be helpful to your analysis. You will want to capture comments made when participants

- Make a navigation choice (why did they make that selection?)
- Begin a new attempt (how did they know they failed?)
- Successfully complete the task (how confident are they?)
- Give up on trying to complete the task (why did they give up?)

Also try to capture any comments along the way that are surprising or telling. Try to capture any unexpected words the participant uses to describe the task, as well as any trigger words the participant is looking for within the content or navigation of your website, especially those words that he or she isn't finding. As you can imagine, these will be helpful comments to discuss during the analysis phase as you think about what changes could be made to your website.

Capture Your Own Thoughts

While both the facilitator and the note taker must outwardly behave as passive, neutral spectators, you will undoubtedly have thoughts racing through your head about what is going on during the test. As you observe someone trying to use your website, you will often think of possible solutions to usability problems you are discovering. As you think of such things, capture these within the notes. Oftentimes, the best ideas can come during the usability test itself, as you are in the midst of the observation. While a more in-depth analysis will come later, those ideas you have at the time should be recorded for inclusion in that later discussion. As you observe participants, think to yourself,

- Why did they click on that?
- Why didn't they click on that?
- Why did they make that decision?
- How could we make this content clearer?
- How could we make this interaction easier?

One way to capture such ideas is to have a standard "What This Means," "Lessons Learned," or "Ideas" section at the end of each task and/or each user session within the notes. In this section, you can capture any ideas the note taker or facilitator thinks of

EXAMPLE OF NOTES

User #1: Undergrad, physics major, never used library website
Task #1: You need to digitize an old document. Find out how.

Attempt #1: Services > Services A–Z > (looked for "digitizing services") - ?

Attempt #2: Help > How do I? > (looked for "digitizing" and "documents") - ?

Attempt #3: Services > Print, Copy Scan ("I think that you scan something to digitize it") > Digitizing collections ("I'm not sure if this is it, but I'll try it") > SUCCESS

Quote: "Ok I think I'm in the right place, although I still don't actually understand how to do this, do I just contact them?"

What this means: Might rewrite the scenario since *digitize* seems to be a trigger word. We should consider adding digitization to the Services A–Z list. Should discuss the whole "How do I" section because a lot of users go here for everything and it doesn't include that much of anything. Maybe we should re-label "Digitizing collections" so it is more clear; not sure. On the page, should make the call to action more clear so the user knows what to do next.

during that session. It is one thing to capture what is happening. It is another thing to capture why you think it is happening and what you hope to do about it.

The facilitator is focused on the moderation of the test and might not have the opportunity to share his or her ideas with the note taker during the test itself. That said, it is important for the facilitator to try and recall these ideas for the debriefing session that will immediately follow. If conducting tests with a number of participants in a row, consider scheduling in a few minutes of reflection in between to allow these ideas to be captured before moving on to the next round.

Identify Success or Failure and Transition to the Next Task

An important element of the usability test, both in note capturing and in moving the test along, is being able to identify success and failure to complete a task. If you clearly defined what successful completion of a task would look like, as described in chapter 5, it should be relatively straightforward as far as when a task is completed successfully. It is possible that the participant completes the task in an unexpected way, using an unexpected navigation path, but a success is a success. Ideally, the participant will succeed at completing a task, possibly after a few attempts, and it will then naturally be time to move on to the next task.

Sometimes, though, the participant will not be able to complete a task, even after numerous attempts. This isn't uncommon, so it is something to be prepared for and to know how to handle. In some cases, a participant might fail to complete a task because there is something technically wrong with the website and it turns out that completing the task is actually impossible. This could be a simple fix, such as a dead link, or could

DOES A PARTICIPANT KNOW IF HE OR SHE IS SUCCESSFUL?

While you will know if a task is completed successfully, it's helpful to know if the participant realizes he or she has completed the task. If the participant isn't confident that the task is actually completed, there could be a usability problem. This is why, in the introduction, you ask participants to let you know when they think they have completed a task.

On occasion, a participant will not be confident that the task is completed and may try to do something else. Once you observe that the task is completed successfully, pause for a few seconds to give the participant time to think and possibly do something else. If the participant appears to be done but has not indicated so, you can ask facilitate the transition by asking, "Do you feel you have completed this task" or "Are you ready for the next scenario?"

be a larger server problem or software updating issue. Either way, the moment that a technical problem such as this is discovered, the note taker should mark the attempt as a failure and the facilitator should move on to directing the participant to complete the next task.

Even without any technical issues, you may find, especially with shorter and more informal usability testing, that a participant will want to give up on completing a task after the first attempt or two. Participants can get frustrated with your website, as can users in real life, and want to just give up. You may have a participant say something like, "At this point, I would just call for help." If you are gathering useful information and this happens, you can ask the participant if he or she would mind trying once more. You can let the participant know that this is very helpful and will help you to make improvements to the website. In some cases, though, you will find that either you are not gathering useful information anymore, or the participant is frustrated enough that it isn't worth the emotional stress to continue the session. When you are in this type of situation, it is OK to allow participants to give up, thank them for their time, and either ask them to complete a different scenario or give them the incentive and let them be on their way.

At the same time, you will have cases where the participant does not necessarily want to give up but is not providing you with any more useful information. This is especially true when a participant attempts to complete the task in the exact same way from one attempt to the next. Most likely, the participant will not consider an alternative way to complete the task and will only continue to be frustrated. If you notice this happening, it is best to end that particular task, have the note taker mark it as failed, and either move

REASONS A TASK MIGHT FAIL

- There are technical problems with the website.
- The participant doesn't have the technical knowledge to complete the task.
- The participant gives up.
- The participant isn't getting any closer.
- You run out of time.

THE EXCEPTION: WHEN YOU CAN GIVE HINTS

Only ever give hints if

1. The participant is hopelessly stuck and is not getting any closer to completing the task.
2. You could gather useful information by having the participant complete that task.

For instance, if you are testing a process that has a number of steps, and the participant is failing to complete a task near the beginning of that process, you might give the person a hint to guide him or her toward the next step. This is necessary in order to gather information about how the participant would complete the rest of the process, once overcoming that initial barrier.

on to the next task or end the session. To do this, simply say something like, "Thank you, this has been very helpful to us. Do you have time to help us with another scenario?" Some facilitators would rather help participants along than have them fail to complete a task, and so will give them hints. This is an option, but will rarely provide you with useful data since the environment is no longer authentic. It also implies to participants that they were, in fact, doing something wrong, and you will show them the correct way to do something. This goes against the idea of being a neutral party. The facilitator is there to observe, watch, and moderate the test, not to guide or advise the participant.

A final case in which a task might fail is when you run out of time. If you are only expecting to spend five minutes with a given participant and he or she has not yet completed the task when you reach five minutes, you may have to end the test. If you are gathering useful information, you can propose the session be extended by saying something like, "This is really helpful. We are at five minutes, but if you have another minute or two to spare, we'd be happy to keep going."

When the participant has either successfully completed or failed to complete the task, it is the job of the facilitator to either transition to the next task or end the session. Be careful not to imply that the participant was wrong or right. If transitioning to the next task, you can say things such as

- "Great, thank you. Let's move on to the next scenario."
- "This has been very helpful. Do you mind trying another scenario for us?"

When participants are no longer on the home page or the page where you would like them to begin the next task, you can direct them to go back to the home page. Alternatively, you can have them stay at whatever web page they happen to be on. In real life, users will often be completing tasks not from the home page, but from internal pages on your website. Consider the goals of the test and facilitate this transition appropriately. Whichever way you choose, try to be consistent in your approach for different participants asked to complete the same tasks.

If it was the final task or you are out of time, you can end the session by saying, "Thank you, this has been very helpful. These are all the scenarios we had for you today."

⊚ End the Test

You want to keep to the time you promised the participants up front. If you advertised a 20-minute test, once you reach the 20-minute mark, let the participants know. If you are still working through a particular task, you may suggest they keep going if they are available, but be sure to let them know they are free to leave.

At the end of the usability test, assuming you have a few minutes to spare, you will have an opportunity to answer any questions the participants might have as well as ask a few of your own final questions. Of course, if you are planning a retrospective review, you should have scheduled in some time at the end to have more in-depth conversation with the participants.

If a participant failed to complete a task, the most obvious question he or she will have is how to succeed in completing the task in the future. If, in fact, the participant will be using your website in real life in the state in which it was tested, it is OK to show him or her how to complete the task right now. It would be poor customer service to not give the person this information. However, as you instruct the participant on how to do something, be clear that you understand it is not very user-friendly right now, and you are going to work on improving it in the future.

Once you have answered any questions from the participants, the facilitator and note taker can then ask any clarifying or probing questions they thought of during the test, but didn't get a chance to ask during the test itself. This is also an opportunity to ask participants for their final impressions. If they have completed a number of tasks, you can ask them about their overall experience and impressions of the website. In shorter tests, it may make more sense to ask participants about their satisfaction or enjoyment level in completing the particular tasks.

If you choose to end by gathering participants' final impressions, consider asking questions such as

- What are your overall impressions of this website?
- How easy or hard did you find it to use?
- Do you feel that you completed the tasks successfully?
- Are you satisfied with the experience you had using this website?
- Do you think you would visit this website again?

The ease in completing a task doesn't always align with the user's satisfaction in completing that task, so it can be helpful to gather this qualitative information from participants to get a fuller picture of the user experience. This can be an additional piece of data to consider during the analysis phase.

When final questions are asked and any final remarks are made, you can give the participants their incentives, thank them, and send them on their way. You have now completed a usability test and, most likely, discovered a number of usability problems with your website.

⊚ Key Points

The actual process of running through a usability test is perhaps the most fun and interesting part of the whole process. This is where you will discover your usability problems by watching actual people using your website. Remember:

- Make the participants feel comfortable.
- Keep the participants talking.
- Manage the participants' emotions.
- Take notes that will help during the analysis phase and be useful to stakeholders.
- Know when to stop the test.
- Be flexible and make adjustments to the test as necessary.
- Practice, practice, practice.

Once completing the usability test, it is time to look at what you found out by analyzing your results and making decisions based on those results.

⑥ References

Krug, Steve. 2010. *Rocket Surgery Made Easy: The Do-It-Yourself Guide to Finding and Fixing Usability Problems*. Berkeley, CA: New Riders.

Rubin, Jeffrey, and Dana Chisnell. 2008. *Handbook of Usability Testing: How to Plan, Design, and Conduct Effective Tests*, 2nd ed. Indianapolis, IN: John Wiley & Sons.

CHAPTER 7

Analyzing Your Findings and Making Improvements

NCE USABILITY TESTING IS COMPLETE, it is time to analyze the results and make some decisions. In this chapter, you will learn how to make changes to your website based on your findings.

⊚ Conduct the Debriefing

It is helpful to meet and discuss what you found out immediately after each usability test, or after a set of back-to-back usability tests. While the experience is fresh in everybody's minds, you will be more likely to recall specific moments, participant comments, and ideas you may have had along the way on how things could work a bit better. Our memories tend to fade, so the sooner you have the debriefing session, the better.

Because of this, schedule a debriefing session immediately after your tests. For example, if you have three usability testing sessions in the morning, schedule a lunchtime discussion about the results. Or if you are organizing half-hour usability tests throughout the day, schedule 15-minute debriefing sessions in between.

The Goals of the Debriefing

The intent of the debriefing session is to reflect upon the user behavior you just observed, identify the usability problems you discovered, and begin brainstorming possible solutions. It is unlikely that you will be able come up with solutions after just one or two usability tests. But as you continue to debrief after each subsequent session, themes will emerge. You will start to notice patterns in user behavior and usability problems that are occurring time and time again. You will also notice some inconsistencies in user behavior, and that not every participant approaches every task in the same way. By conducting numerous tests and continuing to debrief on your findings, your assumptions will be tested and validated, and ideas for solutions will naturally emerge.

Ultimately, you will have a closing debriefing session. Here, you will discuss not only the most recent usability test, but the entirety of the testing process. The goal at this final debriefing session is to have a list of usability problems and a brainstormed list of next steps. The next steps could include an immediate change to your website, a proposed change that you want to test before implementing, more testing to confirm something is, in fact, a problem, and/or a plan to address the problem at a later date.

Who to Invite to the Debriefing

Obviously, you will want at least the facilitator and the note taker to be present at this session. If you had people observing the live test, they should be invited, as well. Sometimes, you will find that the more people, the better (up to a point). By having more people involved, you will be able to get a variety of perspectives on what happened. The disadvantage to only having one facilitator conduct a test and take notes is that the recollection of what happened is all on one person. By having two or more people available to observe, interpret, and analyze the results, you are less likely to reach biased or one-sided conclusions.

At some point, you want to bring stakeholders into the discussion. This can sometimes be done successfully during the debriefing session. While stakeholders who weren't directly involved in observing the test won't be able to contribute their reflections on the

AVOID PREMATURE CONCLUSIONS

You will often find that you simply don't have enough data to make a sound conclusion yet. Avoid jumping to conclusions based on just one or two usability tests, especially if the proposed conclusion might mean a massive change in your website, requiring significant development or design effort. Bring together the data and see where there are gaps and where you need to gather more data. Avoid rushing to make significant changes based on your initial gut reaction.

observation itself, they can hear how things went and share their ideas. If you do this, be careful that stakeholders understand their role and purpose for attending the meeting. Debriefing sessions can be problematic if they become a battle of ideas.

Facilitating the Debriefing

As facilitator for the usability test, you will also likely be the facilitator for the debriefing session. These sessions can become difficult to manage, as people frequently have strong opinions on website design, user behavior, and what a particular observed interaction really meant. Because of this, throughout the debriefing session, be sure to bring the conversation back to the user. Avoid bringing in personal preferences for particular design elements, and ensure that the other people involved do the same. If the session starts to become a battle of personal preferences, step back and say something such as, "Those are both possible solutions. Let's test some more or let's try both solutions out and test again and see what we find out."

⑥ Compile the Raw Data

When conducting a number of usability tests, you will need to compile your results into a cohesive document. Bringing all the data together will allow you to see patterns and start some preliminary analysis. If you are conducting numerous usability testing sessions over the course of a few weeks, it can be helpful to compile your data along the way rather than waiting until after the last session. The compiled data can be useful to have ready for the final debriefing session.

Depending on the amount and type of data you are compiling, you can create a simple written document, or a spreadsheet, or both. It is often helpful to have both in order to capture and manipulate both the qualitative and quantitative aspects of the results. For example, you can have the transcribed notes in a Word document, but supplement it with a spreadsheet that lists each participant, the links selected, the number of attempts, the time on task, and the success rate. This allows you to see the raw qualitative data along with the more structured quantitative data, giving you different ways to look at, discuss, and analyze your findings.

If you used recording software, this is another aspect of data to gather for the analysis. The software may have the ability to synthesize some of the quantitative data for you, perhaps creating a table that gathers number of mouse clicks or time on task. If you have a video recording, you can pull out the most useful or relevant sections of the usability tests to allow for quick review, or attach the relevant video recording to your summary of that session's findings.

As you pull together your data, at minimum you should calculate the following:

- Number of participants
- Percentage of participants who succeeded in completing each task
- Number of attempts it took to complete each task

It can also be useful to measure the following:

- Average time on task for each task (if measured)
- Most-used path to completing the task ("dominant task path")

- Most common navigation elements selected
- Most frequent "wrong turns"
- Most common search terms typed (if applicable)

You may find it helpful to compile this data thoughtfully in a spreadsheet that allows you to search, sort, and filter. Perhaps it will be useful to separate the data out by audience segment, by task, or by date. By having an easy way to manipulate the data, it becomes easier to synthesize and analyze your findings to ultimately get to your recommendations.

Synthesize the Data

You can compile the raw notes and data, but you then want to synthesize your findings in some meaningful way that will allow you to identify usability problems, see overall trends, and subsequently make some decisions. Again, this is a useful resource to have available for the final debriefing session, if possible.

Visualize the Data

Experiment with looking at the data in a variety of ways. Written documents and spreadsheets of data are useful, but there are other, more visual methods to illustrate the data that might prove valuable. For instance,

- Sketch a storyboard of the participants' actions, using thought bubbles and facial expressions for each piece of their journey toward completing the task.
- Draw a flow chart of participants' navigation patterns, illustrating where they went within the information architecture of the site.
- Use mind-mapping software or data visualization tools to see the data from different angles and explore it more deeply.

THE HAWTHORNE EFFECT

As with other types of user research, you need to keep in mind the Hawthorne or "observer" effect, meaning that the very act of observing a test can impact its outcome. Both the observation and facilitation of a usability test is going to alter the results in some way. Because participants are aware that they are being studied, they will not be completely authentic in their interactions with your website. This is one argument for moving away from the think-aloud method, which further impacts the participant's behavior.

It can help to keep the Hawthorne effect in mind as you conduct your analysis, particularly if you encounter behavior that appeared odd or unnatural. For example, participants might spend more time and effort to complete a task within a usability test, whereas in real life they would have given up, asked a friend for help, or used the library's live chat service. Understand that your participants will not behave in exactly the same way that they would out in the real world. This is one of the limitations of usability testing. This does not lessen the value of your results; it is just something to be aware of during the analysis of those results.

Consider your audience and how the data could best be presented for analysis and understanding. Don't be afraid to get creative with how you present the data, especially if you are presenting to a variety of people inside or outside your organization.

Identify Patterns and Themes

It is unlikely that each participant interacted with your website in the exact same way, but it is likely that there were some common trends or patterns. As you compile your results, you will notice commonalities within both the quantitative and the qualitative data.

It should be relatively easy to pull out any overarching themes, especially in the quantitative data. Consider the following:

- What tasks were completed most easily? What was the dominant task path?
- What tasks were the most difficult to complete? How many attempts did they usually take to complete? What was the most common wrong turn?

Table 7.1 is a real example of the quantitative data gathered in a usability test of tasks related to circulation and requesting materials. You can see that 100% percent of participants were able to find information about interlibrary loans within their first attempt. On the other hand, only five out of seven participants were able to successfully request an article, and only 50% of the overall attempts to do so were successful. Even worse, none of the participants were able to successfully suggest a purchase. (In this particular case, only three participants were even asked to complete this task. When all three failed, the facilitator decided to stop including the task since it was obviously such a serious problem.)

Beyond these basic trends, it is important to think critically about patterns in user comments and navigation paths. These will be especially important to your analysis and as you attempt to identify solutions. Did more than one participant

Table 7.1. Example of Compiled Quantitative Data

TASK	NUMBER OF PARTICIPANTS	NUMBER OF ATTEMPTS	SUCCESS RATE BY ATTEMPT	PERCENT SUCCESSFUL BY ATTEMPT	OVERALL SUCCESS RATE	OVERALL PERCENT SUCCESSFUL
Find out circulation periods	6	11	5/11	~45%	5/6	~83%
Find out how to request an interlibrary loan	5	5	5/5	100%	5/5	100%
Find information on fines	5	5	4/5	80%	4/5	80%
Learn how to renew a book	5	8	4/8	50%	4/5	80%
Request an article	7	10	5/10	50%	5/7	~71%
Suggest a purchase	3	10	0/10	0%	0/3	0%

- Use a particular trigger word that wasn't included in the written scenario?
- Go to an unexpected section of the website?
- Use the same unexpected route to complete the task?
- Select the same link or navigation element that took them somewhere they didn't expect?
- Select the browser's back button from the same place?
- Hesitate or express frustration at the same moment during the completion of the task?

When you identify these types of patterns, you are recognizing problematic elements of your website. By paying attention to these commonalities across different users, you will know where on your website to make modifications to address the problems.

Common themes are useful not just for discovering usability problems, but for gaining insight into the user experience more broadly. For instance, did more than one participant

- Comment on the same design element during your home page tour?
- Use the search box in a particular, unexpected way?
- Comment that they would do something differently "in real life" (e.g., search Google, use your university website for a particular task, use Ask a Librarian)?

Identify Significant Comments

Participants' comments make up a large part of the data, so it can be helpful to pull out any comments that were particularly interesting, as well as any comments that were made more than once by different participants. Perhaps participants had similar moments of confusion or hesitation. These can provide you with insight into what participants were thinking when they were attempting to complete the tasks. Quotes can be a powerful tool, and numerous similar quotes from different participants can be especially persuasive and compelling.

Identify Differences between Audience Segments

Throughout your data analysis, pay attention to the similarities and differences between different audience segments, if you were including different audience segments in your usability tests. This is where the participants' answers to the initial interview questions will come into play. For example,

- Did those participants who had used the library or a particular service before behave differently than those who hadn't?
- Were there notably different success rates depending on the participant's background and experiences?
- Did certain participants use different terminology to describe things?
- Was there a correlation between participants' background and the navigation paths they chose?

Understanding how each participant's background influenced their behavior will be helpful in prioritizing usability problems and in identifying solutions. For instance, perhaps

Example 1

Usability tests were conducted for a special collections website. These tests included a home page tour, and in all four cases,

- Participants noticed the large image and spoke positively of it.
- Participants noticed the subject areas for browsing, and were drawn to the red "Explore our collections" button.

Example 2

Participants were asked to find floor maps on the main library website. One hundred percent of participants completed the task, but it wasn't easy. Common navigation patterns were found:

- Six of the seven participants went to "About the Libraries" at least once. This was the first attempt for three participants.
- Three participants went to "University Libraries," but not as a first attempt.
- Three participants went to "Search & Find," but not as a first attempt.

you had great success rates and quick time on tasks for more experienced library users, but found that more attempts were usually necessary for those participants unfamiliar with the library. This might mean that the majority of your current users have few problems completing the primary tasks, but new users require a bit more time to familiarize themselves with a service they haven't used before. This can influence your recommendations to address the usability problems for that particular audience segment.

Create a Summary

With patterns identified, you can create a snapshot of your findings. This snapshot can be used as a basis for your discussions with your web team or any stakeholders during the final debrief, and it is much more useful than a large amount of raw data. A summary can include a table of the quantitative results, such as table 7.1; a list of patterns or trends; and a handful of quotes from participants.

Focus on the Most Problematic Tasks

Many times, you will run across more usability problems than you expected, and more usability problems than you can address in any reasonable amount of time. For this reason, focus your discussions—at least initially—on the most serious of problems. In particular, you want to focus on the tasks that the participants had the most trouble completing. This can usually be determined by simply looking at your overall success rates. Which task, or tasks, had the lowest success rate?

WHAT ABOUT STATISTICAL SIGNIFICANCE?

You could be asked by administrators or stakeholders if your findings are statistically significant and if you can infer that your results would be the same if extended to the larger population. Proving statistical significance is hard because of the human nature of usability testing, and you will almost *never* be able to say with confidence that your data is statistically significant. It will be equally challenging to argue that your results are generalizable to a broader population or a different context. There are simply too many variables to create a truly controlled environment, and it's unlikely you will have the resources to include an actual representative sample of the population. This is especially true in libraries that serve a vastly diverse population.

So when somebody does ask you about statistical significance or generalizability, a good response is that while no, usability testing is not a controlled experiment and it is not feasible to do inferential statistics, you are confident that your results will help you make sound, user-centered decisions. The data you have collected demonstrate that users are having particular problems with your website, and the improvements you make will be appreciated by all subsequent users trying to complete those same tasks.

In addition to success rate, look closely at those tasks that required a considerable number of attempts to complete. Also, pay attention to those areas where participants demonstrated significant confusion or frustration in trying to do something, even if they did ultimately complete the tasks successfully.

Depending upon the complexity of the tasks and the usability (or lack thereof) of your website, you might find that you have few tasks with 100% successful completion, and perhaps no tasks that were completed regularly on first attempt. This doesn't necessarily mean that all of the tasks have usability problems that need to be addressed immediately. Especially as you consider your resource constraints, it is important to focus your time and attention on what matters the most.

The Handbook of Usability Testing provides some detailed approaches on how to prioritize your efforts. The authors tend to use a 70% success criterion: if the success rate of a particular task is below 70%, those tasks are marked as problematic and require attention (Rubin and Chisnell 2008). This can be a helpful general rule as you try to prioritize your problem areas and will help you to focus on the most problematic tasks first. Further, you ought to take into account the severity of the task (i.e., how difficult is it to complete), and the extent of the problem in the real world (i.e., how many users will attempt to complete the task, and how many will probably struggle). Rubin and Chisnell (2008, 261–263) actually have a formula to determine a task's criticality based upon severity and probability:

Criticality = Severity + Probability of Occurrence

Put simply, though, just ask yourself,

- How big of a usability problem is it? Is something completely unusable, or is the problem a stumbling block but most users will overcome it?

Table 7.2. Example of Prioritizing Usability Problems

PROBLEMATIC TASK	PRIORITY	DESCRIPTION
Suggest a purchase	High	No one can find this on the website, and it is a primary task for faculty and graduate students. It is only linked from the faculty research section. We need to put it in a more obvious location.
Request an article	Moderate	Five out of seven participants completed the task, but only half of the overall attempts were successful. This is a primary task for all our audience segments, and we need to make it easier to complete.
Find out circulation periods	Low	Five out of six participants found the information, but it took multiple attempts and they expressed confusion when they reached the page. This is important information for new users, but not for our primary, current users who already know this information. We need to improve the navigation and make the content itself easier to understand, but it isn't a high priority.

- How many users in the real world will this problem impact? How big is the audience segment that would be completing this task, and how many of those users would encounter the usability problem?

You can prioritize your usability problems based upon these criteria. See table 7.2 for an example of high-, moderate-, and low-priority problems based upon severity and probability.

Another way to prioritize the usability problems is by asking the participants themselves where they struggled most and where they think improvements are most needed. This is a question that you can ask as you close out the session with participants and are gathering their final impressions. Their suggestions of priorities may prove useful as you try to determine where to focus your efforts first.

⊚ Focus on the Goals

In addition to gaining insight into the overall usability of your website, there were probably specific things that you wanted to learn by conducting a usability test. Remember that you identified goals for your usability testing, as explained in chapter 4 and 5. What was it that you wanted to learn? What type of data or evidence were you attempting

DON'T LOSE SIGHT OF THE ENTIRE USER JOURNEY

As you try to prioritize your website's usability problems, be sure to consider the full picture. Usability testing has its limitations, and so it can be helpful to reflect upon how your findings translate to users who are actually out in the real world. Perhaps there was some confusion or hesitation by participants who said that they would have used a search engine, used the site search, or asked a librarian in real life. So while usability concerns should not be ignored, these types of instances are perhaps *less* of a problem because those users wouldn't have actually approached a scenario in that particular way *in real life*.

to gather? The things you intended to learn are the things you ought to be focusing on during the analysis.

It is common to discover usability problems on your website that don't directly impact the tasks you were testing. This is often because participants take an unexpected path on your website, or that they point out aspects of your website that you had not paid attention to previously. Certainly, you want to be aware of these usability problems and address them, but these should not be the *focus* of your analysis. They can ultimately distract you from what you were actually trying to test.

⑥ Discover the Root Cause of the Problems

It is one thing to know where participants went wrong in their interaction with your website, but it is a much more challenging thing to know *why* they took the particular paths that they did. To come up with solutions, you need to understand what caused their behavior. What element(s) of the website caused them to make a wrong turn?

Rubin and Chisnell refer to this challenging part as the "source of error analysis" (2008, 260). Identifying the sources of error will guide you to useful solutions. The effort it will take to identify these root causes will vary greatly depending upon the complexity of the tasks and the complexity of your website.

Sometimes, the failure to complete a task is based on a rather obvious technical problem. For example,

- A dead link, or a link that goes to the wrong place
- A function that doesn't work or works incorrectly (e.g., a form that won't submit)
- A software or program issue that prevented the completion of a task (e.g., an out-of-date browser, a disabled plug-in)

When this type of problem is the root cause, the solution is usually equally easy to identify.

More often, though, there isn't something technically wrong with your website or the technology being used to access it, but there is a navigation, design, content, and/or user interface problem. Tackling these types of problems is much more challenging and time-consuming, but it is perhaps the most important part of the entire process. It is going to tell you what caused the usability problem, and subsequently how you can make your website better.

Hopefully, your observation skills, notes, and recording of the session provide you with insight into what your participants were thinking. You should have your list of most problematic tasks. Think critically about each participant's attempt to complete each of those problematic tasks. Identify the problem points during the session. For example, at which points did

- Ginger indicate that she was confused?
- Jeff have to stop and think?
- Rachel select the back button?
- Andrew give up?

For each problematic task, investigate if there was a similar point where most or all of the participants stumbled. Perhaps many of the participants selected the wrong navigation item, indicating that navigation is a core problem. Or perhaps they all went to the correct web page but then hit the back button, not realizing they were on the right track, indicating that the content on that web page is problematic.

Once you have identified some of the key problem points for a given task, dive deeper by asking, "Why?" It can take some investigative work and a critical eye. For example, why did participants

- Select the "University Libraries" menu item? What was their motive? What type of content did they expect this section to provide?
- Not notice the hours on the home page? What were they looking at instead?
- Select the wrong button to submit the form? Why didn't they select the other button?

Figuring out the *why* is no easy feat, and there is not always one correct answer to this question. In fact, there are usually multiple possible answers. This is especially the case for those tasks that took participants numerous attempts to complete, in which each participant took a slightly different route. Similarly, you might have more complicated tasks related to research, requesting materials, or updating account information. These tasks that involve a number of steps can lead you to discover a number of usability problems, with each individual problem having its own source.

⦿ Identify Potential Solutions

Identifying problems is the easy part. Identifying the cause of those problems is trickier. The final step is to now identify solutions. As you can imagine, this is especially challenging work. But the more experience you gain in user-centered design, designing navigation, and writing user-friendly content, the easier this part of the process becomes.

Even if you completed everything up until this point independently, as you get to the solutions phase it is helpful to bring some other people into the conversation. You might facilitate the initial discussion of solutions during the final debrief, or you might need to schedule it later, once you have had some time to synthesize the data and think critically about the problematic tasks and their root causes.

BUT THERE ARE SO MANY PROBLEMS!

As you investigate the *why* of your usability problems, try to focus on what is likely the primary root cause. What is the main source of the problem that seemed to trip the most people up, or caused the most people to go back and start a new attempt? You may notice a number of secondary problems that are associated with the core source of the problem. The same way that you should focus on the most problematic tasks, you should also focus on the primary sources of those problems. Sometimes, by fixing the primary source of a problem, you will inadvertently address those secondary problems, as well. By keeping this focus, you will identify solutions that have the biggest impact and will avoid getting overwhelmed with the extent of the problems you are uncovering.

To identify solutions, if possible, bring in any web developers, designers, or others in your organization who have a knack for problem solving, customer service, and improving the user experience. The developers and designers will bring their technical and user experience knowledge, and others can bring with them a public service mind-set. Together, they can help you think through the various possibilities. They can also ensure that you are identifying solutions that are technically feasible and that are driven by the user experience.

Use Your Instinct

Through synthesizing the data and discussing findings with your colleagues, some possible solutions will naturally come to the surface. In addition to being library staff members, the people in the room are also website users themselves. Some gut reactions and instinct will come into play, and many times that pure instinct can actually be quite valuable. Your instinct can tell you things such as

- If content is difficult to read or understand, which means you need to reorganize, rewrite, or redesign that content
- If buttons or other calls to action are not in an intuitive place, and need to move somewhere more obvious

Use Your Knowledge of Website Usability

As mentioned before, it is extremely helpful to have library staff members with some knowledge of usability or user experience design. This knowledge will play a great part in helping you identify practical solutions to problems. As this knowledge builds within an organization, usability problems become much easier to solve.

If you have a firm grasp of how users interact with websites, you will understand what steps you can take to make your website more usable. A good overview is Steve Krug's classic *Don't Make Me Think* (2000/2014). This should be required reading for anyone building, designing, and maintaining websites. From this book, some basic tenets of user behavior are

- Users don't read pages. They scan them.
- Users don't make optimal choices. They satisfice.
- Users don't figure out how things work. They muddle through.

Because of this, some basic principles of website usability are

- Use conventions.
- Create clear visual hierarchies within your website and individual web pages.
- Make it obvious what's clickable.
- Break up pages into clearly defined areas, allowing them to be easily scannable.
- Omit needless words.

Use Conventions

Library websites are not that unique and should use standard conventions that are immediately recognizable to average website users. Many usability problems arise from design elements that are trying to be flashy or clever, and those problems can often be solved by choosing to use conventional elements instead. These include the following conventions:

- The banner or website logo should take you back to the home page.
- The site search box should be in the top right and should look like a search box.
- Icons should be easily identifiable.

Consider New Navigation Labels

Many times, participants will take an unexpected navigation path, at least initially. This could mean that you need to improve the visual hierarchy on your website in general. It could also be that your website has unclear navigation labels, whether they are primary menu items, tabs, buttons, or links within body text. Perhaps you need to change the label that participants selected, if the content underneath that label was not what participants expected. You might also need to change any labels associated with the intended navigation path to make them clearer. To help you determine what label would be a better option, think about any words you heard participants saying during their attempts. What words were they looking for that weren't there? What navigation element did they click on instead, and why?

Consider Adding (or Removing) Other Access Points

If participants took a variety of different navigation paths in an attempt to complete a particular task, there are two obvious approaches to the problem: make the correct navigation path more intuitive, or make it possible to complete the task through those alternate paths. To make the correct path more obvious, assess your current navigation label(s) and placement. To allow for alternate paths, review those alternate paths and evaluate what that would look like.

Participants will often select broad labels, such as "Frequently Asked Questions," "How Do I . . . ?" and "Services." These tend to be the alternate paths for a number of important website tasks. From a user's perspective, these types of sections on a website can cover nearly any task you can imagine, so it is not surprising that they are regularly selected. However, if a task cannot be completed via these routes, you probably have a usability problem. The obvious solution is to expand upon the content within these broad sections to ensure they cover all your bases. Alternatively, you can avoid having these types of broad sections altogether. This is a particularly sensible option if you have multiple sections like this with different types of content, and those sections are not as comprehensive as they sound.

Consider Rewriting and Reorganizing Content

If participants found the correct place on your website, but then stumbled in actually completing the task, it could be that your content is poorly organized or written within the actual web page. To make improvements, you might

- Remove unnecessary words.
- Write in active voice.
- Restructure and/or rewrite the page headings.
- Shorten paragraphs.

- Use tables, bullets, or numbered lists.
- Use parallelism.

A great resource on learning how to write for the web is Ginny Redish's *Letting Go of the Words: Writing Web Content That Works* (2012). This book is packed with examples of how to write effective web copy, and should be a go-to handbook for anyone who writes content for your website.

Consider Changing Design Elements

If participants failed to see a link or a button, had trouble submitting a form, or failed to read a particular piece of content, it could be that you have design elements that need improvements. It is possible that the entire design theme of your website could be improved. For instance, you could

- Add more white space between paragraphs and/or line breaks, improving readability.
- Adjust your link style so that links are more obviously links, either underlined or distinct from the text by font style and/or color.
- Alter your button design so that buttons are more obviously calls to action.
- Redesign font sizes and colors, including body text and navigation elements.
- Adjust your header style so that headers are clearly headers, are easy to skim, and have more white space above them than below them.

Talk to More Users

As you are thinking through your proposed solutions, it can be helpful to run your ideas by some real users. You don't necessarily have to conduct a usability test again, but you can share the suggested change with some users and gauge their reactions. For example, you can show them a paper prototype of the newly improved web page or conduct some low-tech navigation testing using the new labels. This will give you some more data and can confirm whether you are on the right track toward fixing the problem.

Document Your Recommendations

Once you have identified solutions, document them in a way that will be helpful to your web team and stakeholders. Creating a table that lists the usability problems along with your recommended solutions is a simple, easy way to do this. See table 7.3 for an example of real usability problems that were discovered when testing the hours, location, and parking sections of a website. Some of the proposed recommendations are simple, such as adding entries within the frequently asked questions, and others are more complicated, such as rethinking the entire "Access and Use" section within the primary navigation and moving and redesigning a button associated with library hours.

Identify Small Improvements to Make Immediately

With a list in hand of solutions to your usability problems, you will hopefully find that some changes to your website are easy to implement. These types of changes include fix-

Table 7.3. Example of Usability Problems and Recommendations

USABILITY PROBLEM	RECOMMENDATIONS
Participants went to "Frequently Asked Questions" (FAQ) to find out about hours, locations, and parking.	• Add FAQ entries about hours (what are the library hours?), locations (where are the library locations/branches?), and parking (where and how can I park?)
Participants went to "Access and Use" for information on hours, locations, and parking.	• Re-label "Access and Use" to better represent the content that lives there, or remove it entirely from the primary navigation and place it within the "Policies" section.
Participants didn't know they could click on the clock icon to get to hours information.	• Redesign the button so it looks more like a button, • Add text to the button that says "Hours." • Move the button closer to "Today's hours" so it is more clearly associated with the hours.

ing dead links or functionality, changing navigation labels, or improving content within a single web page. Other proposed solutions will be much more complicated. They can include restructuring a larger section of your website, changing the global navigation, or improving and entire workflow for a complicated, multistep process.

A common mistake is to not make a change either because it is too much work or because a better solution is coming down the road. Ultimately, you should aim to make improvements to address every problematic task you discovered on your website. These improvements may require significant design, development, or content work. While you might not have the resources to make the improvement that is really needed, is there a more minor improvement you could make *right now* that could make a difference? Usually, there is.

For example, you could find out that it is very difficult to search for streaming films within your discovery tool, and that this is due to inconsistent catalog records. You would like to make improvements to the metadata in your catalog records, allowing users to limit their search to online films more seamlessly, but that would be a massive cataloging project. Rather than not doing anything, consider what you can do. What is the easiest way for users to find streaming films, and how can you direct them there? Perhaps you can use some customization options to direct users to a particular database rather than having them search within the discovery tool. Or perhaps you can make a scoped search

EXAMPLE OF NEWS AND EVENTS

In usability testing, it was discovered that participants had a hard time finding and navigating the library's news and events information, which was scattered in different locations. A library project was underway to rebuild the entire news and events application, bringing the content together and making it more visual, navigable, and user-friendly. This was many months out, though, so in the meantime the web team created a page titled "News and Events." This new page brought together the disconnected content into one place. While it wasn't the ideal result, it was a good interim solution until the larger project made the more comprehensive improvements.

box using a variety of more complicated search filters and embed it in a logical place on your website.

Seemingly small improvements can still have a big impact. Try to avoid falling into the trap of waiting for a more robust solution. There is often a better, more comprehensive solution down the road, but you will have many website visitors in the meantime. If there is something small you can do that will have big impact, do that now. It might be creating a web page, updating a link, or redirecting users to a useful alternative. It is better to make a small improvement that will make things a bit easier for many users now than it is to just wait for something that might happen down the road.

Identify Bigger Improvements for Down the Road

It's true that library websites are often very complicated, and you will likely find usability problems that you cannot fully address any time soon. These types of problems will regularly involve outside products, such as research databases and integrated library systems.

You may find that there are internal processes that cause usability problems on your website, and that improvements cannot be made until the internal processes are adjusted. For instance, it could be that users expect to see both their regular and interlibrary loan books within a single account, but your library manages these through two different accounts within two different departments.

It is good to identify those larger problems and create a plan for implementing some larger scale solutions down the road. These larger solutions may involve a number of components, such as

- Updating internal processes (e.g., how book requests are managed)
- Updating collection records or metadata (e.g., material types or descriptions)
- Making recommendations to vendors (e.g., interface changes within research databases)

Again, you want to make the smaller improvements that you have the ability to make now. But don't overlook those larger, underlying issues or let them slip through the cracks. While these larger scale changes can require significant time and effort, they can make even more significant improvements to the user experience. Set a plan of action on moving toward these more comprehensive solutions in the long term. Your users will thank you for it.

Remember the Other Themes

Beyond usability problems, usability testing will provide you with a wealth of other interesting and useful information about your users. These are themes that will come out during your initial synthesis of the data. Perhaps you heard thought-provoking comments and learned something unexpected. While the focus during the analysis is on fixing the problems, don't forget about all the other things you learned.

For example, you may have found that participants overwhelmingly reacted positively to a particular design element, or weren't aware of a particular service the library offers, or commented on what they would have done "in real life." These aren't usability problems,

Table 7.4. Example of Themes and What They Mean

THEME	WHAT THIS MEANS
Participants liked the image on the home page.	We should keep the image on the home page and have a rotating selection.
Participants didn't know about our digital collections, but were excited when they saw that we had them.	We need to promote our digital collections more prominently and make them more discoverable.
Participants mentioned that they would use Ask a Librarian when they couldn't find something.	Ask a Librarian is a useful service, and people like using it. We should continue to make it easily available on the website.

but are important nonetheless. They can lead to better understanding of your users and help guide some longer term efforts at your organization. Table 7.4 illustrates how you can compile this type of data in a table that lists the themes along with what they mean for the library.

Test Again (Sometimes)

Especially if you are new to usability testing, it is a good idea to conduct subsequent tests to confirm that the recommended change actually fixed the problem, or at minimum improved the experience from previously. To do this, it is important to try to control the usability study so that other factors don't influence your findings. Specifically,

- Keep the same scenarios as they were written the first time.
- Recruit the same number of participants with similar backgrounds (but never use the *same* participants, since their previous participation will influence their behavior).
- Use the same technology.
- Use the same facilitator.
- Only change the thing on the website you want to test. Don't change other, unrelated things that could unintentionally impact user behavior.

Once the subsequent usability tests are completed, compile the data in the same method used with the initial test. It ought to be pretty straightforward to compare the data from the initial study to the second study. If your success rate increased, then you can say with confidence that your recommended solution did in fact address the usability problem. If your success rate decreased or remained the same, it is time to go back to the drawing board and come up with an alternate solution.

In some cases, a subsequent test isn't necessary. When you have resource constraints, it is sometimes better to just implement a change rather than spend the staffing resources to continue with testing. Be cautious with this, and only implement a change without retesting when you can say with certainty that it will not make the situation any worse and can only make it better. For example, in a usability test it was found that a participant selected a button titled "Calendar," expecting that it would display a calendar of hours. In fact, it displayed a calendar of library events. To address this usability problem, the web team renamed the button "Event Calendar." This was a minor change that made the label much clearer, and a subsequent test was not necessary to prove that point.

Figure 7.1. The Testing Life Cycle.

◎ The Testing Life Cycle

You may benefit from establishing a testing life cycle for your most problematic tasks. As figure 7.1 illustrates, you can make improvements after each usability test, continuing to test and ensure your website is increasingly meeting the needs and expectations of users. This allows you to continually make improvements to your website and adjust things as user behavior evolves and your services expand.

You will find a testing life cycle especially helpful when you are testing complicated tasks with multiple steps, such as the interlibrary loan process or the process for renewing materials. In your initial recommendations, you might focus on fixing the most problematic parts of the process. In subsequent usability tests, you may notice other usability problems that need addressing. Over time, your success rate should continue to increase as you make the process more seamless and easy for the user.

Similarly, you should implement a testing life cycle for those important tasks that involve tools that are regularly changing. For instance, your library catalog or web-based discovery tool will continue to add new content and features, so it is important to continue to test those tools with real users.

◎ Share Your Findings

Create a Written Report

Your organization might be interested in seeing a full report of your findings. This may or may not be necessary in your circumstances, but a usability testing report is a helpful way to formally document what you found. This can prove useful in justifying decisions and can be a helpful resource in the future for tracking historical decisions, changes in user patterns, and longer term trends. These reports also provide you with data that demonstrate how decisions based on usability testing have positively impacted the user experience over time. This helps prove the value in usability testing.

The full report of your findings should include

- A statement about the goals of the usability testing
- An outline of how the testing was conducted, including recruitment efforts, technology used, and people involved
- A list of the tasks that were included in the testing, along with the scenarios that were read to the participants
- The synthesized findings, including tables of quantitative data (e.g., table 7.1), big themes and patterns, useful quotes from participants, and any differences in behavior between audience segments
- Your list of usability problems and recommended solutions (e.g., table 7.3)
- Your list of any other themes and what they mean for the library (e.g., table 7.4)

This type of report can be a detailed document spanning several pages, or it can be just a page or two, depending on the extent of usability testing conducted as well as your audience and the intention of the report.

Consider Your Audience

There are a number of purposes to the final report, but primarily, it serves as a communication tool. It can educate stakeholders on how the process works, raise awareness of usability problems, and justify your decision making. As you write the report, consider your audience and what they will find most useful, interesting, or compelling. If the report is going to be used by the web team as a historic account of your detailed findings, you could benefit from having two versions: a detailed report for your web team and a summarized report to share broadly with library staff. You can find an example of a complete summary report in the appendix.

Present Your Findings in Person

In-person presentations and meetings with stakeholders are often more effective than a written report alone. A real-time discussion will allow you to make sure the synthesized data is understandable and will allow stakeholders to ask any clarifying questions. You can also use the opportunity to discuss your recommended solutions and gather any feedback and concerns from other staff members.

Take advantage of the in-person format. If you have a recording of the usability tests, this is a great opportunity to share clips from those recordings that are particularly compelling and demonstrate the problems you have identified. You can also use the presentation format to share your tables of quantitative data as well as any interesting data visualizations. Further, you can share series of screenshots that demonstrate the paths participants took in order to complete the tasks.

By organizing this type of presentation, you will gain interest and enthusiasm from library staff members. You will raise awareness of usability problems and gain support for continued usability testing and improvements to your website.

⊚ Make Decisions and Implement Changes

Hopefully, your recommended solutions will be implemented relatively soon after usability testing is complete. There can be a few steps in between, though, depending on your situation. For instance, you may need to have a conversation with the appropriate library staff members to ensure the solution is practical and sustainable. These conversations can involve web developers, designers, or content providers. You also might need to identify the library staff members who are able to implement the changes, and perhaps talk with their supervisors to receive approval that time can be dedicated to doing the work.

In addition to figuring out *what* needs to be done and *who* needs to do it, you will need to figure out *when* it can be done. The speediness in which you are able to implement your recommended changes to your website will depend on a number of factors, for instance,

- Who has decision-making authority? Who has to "approve" the recommendations?
- What is your organization culture like? How adapt are library staff to changes like the ones you are proposing?
- What resources do you have to actually implement the changes? What staff are available that have the skill sets to make the changes, and what kind of time do they have?
- What else will be impacted by the change and are there any dependencies? Do you need to first fix links or make other updates elsewhere on the website or in dependent applications?
- Whose work will be impacted by the change? Who needs to know about the upcoming change, and how much advanced warning do you need to give them? Do you need to make the change available for library staff to review and become familiar with it before it goes live?

In chapter 8, you will learn about ongoing usability testing and building workflows so that, among other things, the implementation of recommended changes is a clear, practical, and nimble process.

⊚ Key Points

Making sense of your findings from usability testing is not always easy, but it is essential. It is the entire reason that you conduct usability testing in the first place. Data becomes pretty meaningless if you don't know how to use it or what to do with it. Remember:

- Debrief as soon as you can with the facilitator, note taker, and any observers.
- Focus on trends and patterns across different participants.
- Focus on the most serious problems, and don't forget the original goals of the usability test.
- Discuss what they did, and focus on the *why* of what they did.
- Identify the small and the big changes that would improve the usability of the website.
- Test again, as possible, and develop a testing life cycle for the most problematic or complicated tasks.

- Share your findings with stakeholders.
- Make sound decisions and quickly implement changes to your website.

You have now been guided through each piece of the usability testing process, from planning to execution and analysis. Next, you will learn how to create a process for ongoing usability testing, establishing a commitment from your library organization and building it into your ongoing work.

References

Krug, Steve. 2000/2014. *Don't Make Me Think, Revisited: A Common Sense Approach to Web Usability*. 3rd ed. Berkeley, CA: New Riders.

Redish, Janice (Ginny). 2012. *Letting Go of the Words: Writing Web Content That Works*. 2nd ed. Waltham, MA: Morgan Kaufmann.

Rubin, Jeffrey, and Dana Chisnell. 2008. *Handbook of Usability Testing: How to Plan, Design, and Conduct Effective Tests*. 2nd ed. Indianapolis, IN: John Wiley & Sons.

Ongoing Usability Testing

USABILITY TESTING IS USEFUL IN ANY CAPACITY, but ongoing, programmatic usability testing is by far the most effective way to ensure you are continually providing a good user experience. Nothing is static: not content, technology, or the services and resources that you provide. As your website changes and technology evolves, there will be a continual need to ensure that your website is usable and enjoyable.

Usability Testing for Something New

Oftentimes, you will hear about usability testing as part of the process for creating something new. Perhaps you need to build a website for an entirely new library, consortium, or association. Or perhaps there is a new library branch, repository, or digital collection that requires its own website. If you are involved in the creation of an entirely new website, you will want to build usability testing into the process.

More often, you won't be creating an entirely new website, but you will be making something new within an existing website. It could be that your library is developing a new product, service, or resource. This can be something as significant as a new discovery tool or account management system. It can also be relatively minor, such as a new blog or online exhibit.

In much of the library literature, you will read about usability testing of web-based discovery tools, such as Summon, Primo, and Ebsco Discovery Service. This is especially true given the growth and prevalence of these systems in recent years. Occasionally, you will see usability testing results from other new services, such as room reservations. Regardless of the scope, you can incorporate usability testing into the process to ensure the new thing is usable by the intended audience.

In the context of creating something new, you can build usability testing into the process in a variety of ways. You can test during any or all of the following phases:

- The initial mock-ups of the concept, possibly using paper prototypes or static wireframes rather than a live website
- The navigation elements of the website with minimal content other than that which relates to the primary tasks
- A staging or development website that contains select content
- The final product before launch
- The product after launch

All too often, usability testing isn't conducted until the new service or product is already launched and being used by actual website visitors. Ideally, you want to build usability testing into your development process and conduct at least *some* level of testing before launch to avoid encountering serious usability problems. In some cases, though, you will be limited, and testing postlaunch is certainly better than not testing at all.

Usability Testing for a Website Redesign

Usability testing is perhaps even more common within the context of a website redesign project. These large-scale projects are commonplace, and the purpose is not usually to

WHY NOT JUST DO USABILITY TESTING WHEN IT'S LIVE?

When you are unveiling a brand-new service, resource, or product, you often want to get it out there as quickly as possible. It's a new and exciting thing. At the same time, you want it to be well received. One or two bad experiences can deter users from ever trying to use it again. For this reason, it's important to try to test things before they go live. This will give you greater confidence in providing a good user experience. If it's not feasible to do usability testing before something goes live, you might want to indicate that the new thing is "beta" or "in development" so that users understand it is not yet in its final iteration. You should then conduct usability testing of the live product and make tweaks based on your results. Additionally, you should encourage users to submit feedback and then make improvements based on the feedback you receive.

unveil something *new*, but rather to improve the website that already exists. These projects tend to require several months or even a year or more of work, involving user research, meetings with stakeholders, information architecture development, content reviews and updates, mock-ups of the new website, and eventually the major relaunch.

Usability testing is a part of every good redesign project. It is sometimes built into the final stages of the project before launch, when it is in a "final draft" form. Other times, it is incorporated throughout the entire design and development process. Ideally, you want to use the latter approach: conduct usability testing at all stages of the project, from before the start of the project to after the launch of the new site. This will allow you to catch usability problems more quickly and ensure you are meeting the needs of users every step of the way. This type of iterative development has become popular in recent years, and arguably is the best way to approach a redesign effort.

Website Redesign Is Not Always the Answer

That said, website redesigns have become less popular in general, and are not always (or even *usually*) the answer to your website woes. Historically, institutions have put significant funding into website redesign projects, but haven't built the infrastructure to then maintain and iterate on those new websites. All too often, especially for libraries that have small if any web design and development staff, redesign efforts are contracted out to web design firms. These expert design teams can conduct usability testing as part of their process, perhaps inviting library staff to join in, and can create great websites that provide an excellent user experience. Yet, once the website is launched, the library staff doesn't have the tools, people, or workflows in place to keep it going. Websites being what they are, they eventually become problematic. Perhaps content becomes outdated and inconsistent, design elements don't meet the new brand, and the site isn't accessible on new types of mobile devices. Needless to say, a few years later, library staff and administrators find themselves again talking about the need for a redesign. So the redesign is then repeated again and again, every few years. This model of focusing effort on your website just once every few years is clearly unsustainable. It doesn't treat websites as the ever-evolving entities that they are, and doesn't give them the attention that they deserve.

So, not surprisingly, the iterative approach to website development has become the new thinking among leaders in the field. This means that an ongoing effort to improve your website, and a commitment to website development, is a better approach than only focusing effort on the website every few years with a massive redesign.

Ultimately, you want to build an ongoing, institutional commitment to your website. You want to allow your website to be adaptable to new user needs, institutional priorities, and technology. If the support and infrastructure is there, you will be continuously making improvements, iterating design, rethinking content, and improving the technical infrastructure and systems to support it all. If done well, redesign may never be necessary again.

Sometimes Website Redesign Is Necessary

The world is not quite ready for the end of website redesigns. For many libraries, a redesign is the only option when things haven't been maintained over the years. You may have serious usability, content, and technical problems with your website, perhaps problems so overwhelming that the only logical thing to do is start over completely. You also might have a technical requirement, such as an institutional move to a new content management system, which requires not only redesigning but *rebuilding* your entire website.

In 2014, website redesign projects remain commonplace and are often the only feasible option. Because of neglect, library websites are all too often in dire need of a massive overhaul. A big redesign project will allow you to start from scratch. And if done well, perhaps your latest redesign will be the last one of its kind you will ever have to undertake.

Usability Testing during the Redesign

As said earlier, usability testing is part of every good redesign project. When you are undertaking massive changes to your information architecture, content, and design elements, it is important to build usability testing into various stages in the process. It is OK to test something that is incomplete. Avoid waiting until the last moment to test something important.

During a redesign project, you can start conducting usability testing during the initial planning stages:

- Test your current website to find out where it succeeds and where it fails in order to learn what you should keep the same and what needs major improvements.
- Test comparable websites you might want to model after to help you decide upon labels, navigation elements, and content.

Also, conduct usability testing during all stages of development and iteration:

- Once you have a first draft of navigation and draft content, test the findability of the most important content (this can be done with paper prototypes).
- Once you have all the elements to complete primary tasks, test those primary tasks and iterate until you receive high success rates.

Further, conduct usability testing in preparation for the major launch:

- When you are ready to launch (or so you think), test the full version of the website to ensure the primary tasks are still easy to complete.

Finally, conduct usability testing after the major launch:

- Confirm things are working in production as well as they worked in the staging or development website.
- Build a process for ongoing usability testing and improvements.

Use an Iterative Approach

Regardless of your views on the worth of website redesigns, libraries and library websites are constantly changing. Content evolves. Services change. Resources expand in format and scope. Technology is a moving target. In recent years, there has been an explosion of e-books and e-readers, search and discovery tools, and citation management systems. The types of services that libraries are providing to users are continually expanding in some ways and narrowing in others, as libraries figure out the new role they play in society and how they can best serve their communities.

So while a redesign is sometimes the only answer to your website problems, the effort should never stop there. An iterative approach to website improvements is your best bet. So, rather than conducting usability testing for an isolated period of time, such as during a website redesign project or as a new service is being developed, figure out a way to conduct iterative usability testing: as needed and appropriate. This allows you to be more nimble and flexible in changes to your website, and will ensure that your website continues to stay usable, enjoyable, and accessible to your audience.

Figure Out What and When to Test

The best way to build an organizational commitment to ongoing usability testing is to clearly define *when* you will test *what*, and then hold yourself accountable to doing it. Unless you have a very small website or a very large staff, you will never be able to test absolutely everything. You already know it is important to test the tasks that are most important to users. But beyond that, at what moments is it most important to test your website's usability? And when are you (and others) available to actually do it?

A combination of approaches might work best. Build an ongoing effort by testing substantial changes, testing things that are new, testing existing issues, and testing on a schedule. To support all of these things, you need to also build in processes and workflows to make it happen.

Test Substantial Changes

Consider the types of changes you make to your website. You want to make sure that any significant changes you make are improving the user experience or, at minimum, not making things any worse. Naturally, usability testing is a great way to find this out. But since you cannot test every single instance of change, what type of changes are *substantial* enough that they should require some form of usability testing before implementing?

A great way to ensure ongoing commitment to usability is to test all substantial, high-impact changes before those changes are made live. In order for this to work, you will need to build definitions to clearly distinguish between those *substantial* or high impact changes versus more common *maintenance* or low-impact changes. For example, substantial changes can be defined as

- Adding or removing global navigation elements (e.g., primary navigation, footer)
- Adding or removing content from the home page
- Creating a new web page
- Significant edits to one of the most commonly used web pages

Other types of changes can be considered maintenance, low-impact changes. These may not require usability testing, although they should require some other type of structured workflow. Maintenance changes can be defined as

- Content editing within a web page
- Deleting a web page with low usage

- Creating a particular type of new content (e.g., news story, entry in the staff directory)

The exact definitions may vary, depending upon your institution, your staffing, and the website in question. However you define them, by distinguishing between these types of changes you will be able to focus your efforts on those changes that have the most impact on users. This approach has a number of benefits. By committing to usability testing on substantial changes, it will

- Keep you accountable for doing ongoing usability testing by documenting this commitment in writing
- Get stakeholders on board with larger changes, since you will have data to back up those decisions
- Build trust among stakeholders and users that you know what you're doing, since you are paying attention to what is important and making changes that have positive impact

Test Things That Are New

Further, you might want to commit to usability testing of all things new. Perhaps a new service is being introduced to users, such as the ability to reserve rooms, pay late fees online, or get text message notifications. As discussed earlier, these are great opportunities to do usability testing.

If possible, you could make it a policy, or at minimum a recommendation, that *all* new services go through some form of usability testing before being offered. Perhaps the teams responsible for new services build a user research component into their process, and this becomes a routine element before launching anything new.

In reality, this might not always be practical as you want to push new services out as soon as possible. If this is the case, perhaps you can establish a rule that usability testing will be conducted within the first two months or so of the service being offered. Many times, there is excitement about a new service by both library staff and users, so you might have some vested interest in doing this and support from stakeholders. If conducting usability testing prior to the service being offered, you may also find very willing participants who want to get a "sneak peek" at the new, exciting service that will soon be offered.

Test Things Discovered during Previous Usability Tests

As mentioned in the previous chapter, you will likely discover usability problems that you can't address right away. Because of this, you need to be sure to keep a historical record of what happened during a usability test and what usability problems you encountered. You will find problems not associated with your goal for testing or too big to tackle at this point in the game. While you might set these problems aside, you do not want to ignore or forget about them.

A simple approach to doing this is to keep an evolving list of problems along with previously gathered data about each particular issue. By recording these problems in a structured way, you will have a list of other things to test. You can prioritize this list based upon impact to users as well as your ability to address the problems. From this list, you can develop new tasks and scenarios for testing.

OTHER BENEFITS OF KEEPING A HISTORICAL RECORD

By keeping track of known issues and possible things to test, you will gain insight into usability problems in general and will begin to strengthen the knowledge in your organization. Based on historical problems you have found, you might create some usability standards to avoid having similar problems in the future. For instance, if you find that your link style is difficult to read or unnoticeable for many users (it blends into the rest of the text, for instance), you should change the style to something more obvious, test that it works, and implement this standard style across your website.

Test Things Discovered through Other Methods

Library assessment tools such as surveys, focus groups, and feedback forms can be great opportunities to find out problems related to the user experience. Oftentimes, there will be direct and easy correlations with your website. Perhaps users are complaining about your search tool or catalog, confusion about services, or technical issues they have encountered.

A user experience, assessment, or public services department can track these types of comments, suggestions, and complaints from customers. Many of them can turn into new tasks for usability testing. They can be integrated into the list of problems you are creating as you conduct usability tests. Similarly, they can be prioritized based on both impact to users and your ability to address the problems.

Test on a Schedule

In addition to testing when things are new or changing, you need to ensure that you have the time set aside to actually do the testing. It is all well and good to say that you commit to something, but if the time is not set aside to do it, you will find yourself too busy and will unintentionally break your commitment.

So, it is helpful to also commit to usability testing on a regular, scheduled basis. In *Rocket Surgery Made Easy: The Do-It-Yourself Guide to Finding and Fixing Usability Problems*, Steve Krug (2010) advocates for testing one morning a month. The key is to creating a schedule that you can actually follow, so depending on your staffing and method chosen for testing, it can be more or less often than this. Consider your schedule and staffing availability, and availability of participants for recruitment. However you schedule testing in, by building this into your work schedule, you will be much more likely to stick to it.

It helps to have all members of your web team build testing into their work schedules. You can keep an ongoing list of tasks and test different tasks each month, or retest tasks that had low success rates after you made a change to hopefully address the usability problem.

By testing on a schedule, you will experience a number of benefits, including

- Keeping you accountable since you have set the time aside and it is on your calendar

- Providing you with ongoing, regular practice, allowing you to improve your skills and streamline the process
- Allowing you to react quickly based on your results

Create a Process, Workflows, and Infrastructure

You might have the best intentions to do everything just mentioned. You plan to test often and test systematically. Yet, time has a tendency to get away from you. Other work takes priority, and there simply isn't the time for this kind of ongoing commitment. Additionally, you aren't really accountable to anyone, except maybe yourself, so things can easily fall through the cracks.

To address this problem, create a real process for it. Establish documented workflows and schedules for when usability testing will take place and who will be responsible for doing it. This may involve a policy document that states that usability testing is required in X and Y cases before a change can happen, or before a new service can be put into practice.

At the University of Arizona Libraries, a document was created on the process for website changes. In this document, "substantial," "maintenance," and "unexpected" changes were defined. Examples were given for each. In each section was the following:

- An explanation of who might identify the need for change and how he or she is expected to communicate that need
- A process for gathering feedback from stakeholders
- A definition of who has decision-making authority to approve of the change
- A statement on how the change will be prioritized within other work commitments
- A process for communicating the change to stakeholders
- An expectation of if and when usability testing will be conducted and how

This document grew as new websites were added, new examples were brought to the surface, and responsibilities and workflows became more clearly established. Because libraries can often be complex organizations with numerous websites, stand-alone applications, locations, and stakeholders, a documented process for changes and updates can become quite extensive if it is to capture all possible examples.

As you create such processes, be cautious that they don't become barriers to innovation and flexibility. You don't want usability testing to be seen as a roadblock to getting things done. This can be a balancing act, and it might be that your initial process needs to be tweaked as it is put into practice.

The goal is to get people within your organization both excited about usability testing and *committed* to actually doing it. Some ideas on how to keep up the energy and excitement around usability testing are discussed in the final chapter.

Adapt to Your Environment

All organizations are different, and there is no one approach to ongoing usability testing. Be thoughtful about how you build usability testing into your work and your organiza-

DEVELOP A CONTENT STRATEGY

An incredibly important part of a website is its content. The quality of the content can make or break a website's usability. A content strategy involves the establishment of standards, workflows, roles, and responsibilities related to content. A solid content strategy will include processes for the creation, updating, and deletion of web content of all types. Done well, it will ensure the usefulness, usability, and findability of your web content now and into the future. For more on content strategy, read Kristina Halvorson's *Content Strategy for the Web* (2012).

tional culture. Undoubtedly, you will have to adjust your plan along the way as you put it into practice. You will learn what works and what doesn't, and should remain open to different approaches as time goes on.

Consider the People

Ongoing usability testing requires people committed to doing it. You are more likely to sustain an ongoing commitment if you have the right people in the right roles. The more people involved, the more likely you are to be successful. Consider the following:

- Who is a strong advocate for improving the user experience and can be a usability champion within your organization?
- Who enjoys this type of work?
- Who is good with people?
- Who is a good problem solver?
- Who is good at doing which pieces of the work—facilitating the test, capturing notes, analyzing results, and coming up with recommendations?

In the final chapter, there is discussion about putting someone in charge. In addition to putting the right person in charge, you also have to put the right staff members in supporting roles. In a best-case scenario, you will have not just one person dedicated to usability testing, but a small team of people. These people can perhaps work across different departments and have different levels of expertise, bringing their various skill sets and perspectives to the table.

In some cases, staff members conducting usability testing will come and go. This is especially true if you are asking student workers or volunteers to do some of this work. For ongoing testing to be successful, you need to have a plan for recruiting and training new people to come on board as needed.

So, in order to maintain informed, energized, and committed people to doing the work, consider

- Incorporating usability testing into job descriptions and performance evaluations
- Forming a group of people who are engaged, passionate, and skilled at usability testing

- Rewarding people who demonstrate their commitment to the user experience
- Creating a basic training plan and training resources for new people

Consider the Support

For a process to work effectively, you have to have the right people, and those people need to be given the tools to be successful. They need to feel supported by their supervisors and administrators. A true commitment will involve an ongoing dedication of resources—both time and money—to the effort.

In a best-case scenario, the time to do the work should be clearly allocated within job descriptions and staff held accountable through a performance review process. Perhaps you even have dedicated positions such as *user research specialist* or *user experience librarian*. If nothing else, you can recognize the work within annual performance goals or objectives. It might be that this starts off small and evolves over time as your institution learns the value of usability testing and dedicates more human effort to the cause.

Further, you should advocate for some level of fiscal commitment. This could be a small sum of money set aside for assessment or user research that can be tapped into for usability testing. Again, you might need to start off small. Perhaps you request one-time money in the amount of $50 to do a few rounds of usability testing using an informal, intercept recruitment method. Growing upon that, you can try to advocate for $1,000 of the annual budget to use a more formal recruitment method. This amount can be small in the scheme of things but can go a long way to providing incentives to participants.

You also will benefit from purchasing appropriate hardware and software. Again, starting out small, you might ask for a tablet to take out in the field along with some type of screen-capturing software. Longer term, you might want to create a permanent, formal usability lab within your library space. This can be a former meeting or study room that is transformed into a quiet space dedicated to usability testing sessions. It could include a variety of computers, software, and recording devices, and may also include an observation room next door.

If you are unable to get much commitment in the form of time or money, you might need to pull back on your approach. Perhaps instead of testing every month, you can only test quarterly. Or perhaps instead of doing formal recruitment, you need to just do some on-the-fly intercept usability testing for the time being. This might not be ideal, but it might be the best option if you are lacking the institutional support. Remember that *some* usability testing is always better than *no* usability testing.

Consider the Culture

Organizational cultures can play a big role in this, as well. In cultures where library staff members are already making user-centered decisions and advocating for an improved user experience, it can be relatively easy to build new processes in support of usability testing. In other, more traditional environments, this can be more of a challenge.

The likelihood of being able to successfully integrate usability testing into current workflows is going to depend greatly on organizational norms. In a more flexible and agile culture, you might be able to more quickly and easily build usability testing into your workflows. In a more process-oriented culture, you might have to start to build a solid case and slowly gather support from administrators before you are given institutional support to move the effort forward and actually put something in place.

Consider Decision-Making Authority

The results of usability testing can inform significant changes to your website, but who is responsible for making those important decisions? In smaller organizations, it might be an easy thing to update your website's navigation, home page, or design. But in larger, more complex organizations, these types of decisions will need to be vetted with the appropriate stakeholders. In your library, who has responsibility for what types of decisions related to your website? If this is unclear, who can you talk to in order to begin those discussions?

Creating documented standards, processes, and workflows related to website changes will be of great benefit as you move to an iterative approach. These documents should include decision-making authority when it comes to website modifications, and will likely evolve over time as new approaches are integrated and responsibilities are established. As you establish a usability testing program, you will need to have a clear understanding of whether you are making decisions or recommendations based on what you find out. This will allow you to move on the proposed website changes in a way that helps users while following appropriate communication channels at your institution.

Key Points

Usability testing is all too often done as a one-time effort or sporadically, either as part of a website redesign or as part of a new venture. While it's important to conduct usability testing in these cases, the most successful library websites will involve strategic, ongoing usability testing. Remember:

- Usability testing should be an integral part of designing new services, resources, and products.
- Website redesigns are not a sustainable answer to your usability problems, but are sometimes your only option and should always include usability testing.
- Take an iterative approach to improving your website and you might never have to redesign again.
- Commit to usability testing, and hold yourself accountable to that commitment.
- Create infrastructure to support your commitment.
- Be flexible and create a method appropriate to your institution.

You are hopefully excited about creating a usability testing program at your institution, but how do you keep up the momentum? In the final chapter, you will learn methods for how to do just that.

References

Halvorson, Kristina. 2012. *Content Strategy for the Web*. 2nd ed. Berkeley, CA: New Riders.
Krug, Steve. 2010. *Rocket Surgery Made Easy: The Do-It-Yourself Guide to Finding and Fixing Usability Problems*. Berkeley, CA: New Riders.

CHAPTER 9

Keeping Up the Momentum

IN THIS CHAPTER

Find out

▷ Why assigning responsibilities is key to continued success with usability testing

▷ How ongoing, strategic communication will help your cause

▷ Why fostering a culture of user experience will spread the work around and make staff resources less of an issue

▷ Why you, and others conducting usability testing, must commit to continual learning

▷ What other user research methods are available to help guide your website decisions

WHILE THERE ARE MANY METHODS for ongoing testing, it is essential to keep up the momentum in your library in order to sustain these methods over time. In this chapter, you will learn how to establish responsibilities to ensure usability testing gets done, communicate the value of testing, and foster a culture that puts user experience first. You will also learn about the importance of continuing to stay on top of trends, research, and tools related to user experience, and get briefly introduced to other user research methods that can be of benefit beyond usability testing.

Put Someone in Charge

In order to make ongoing usability testing a reality, somebody in your organization needs to be dedicated to it. It needs to be within someone's job description in order for usability testing to be conducted in a sustainable and ongoing way, using processes described in the previous chapter. If nobody is held accountable for usability testing, it is likely that it will fall down the list of organizational priorities and simply won't get done.

In larger library organizations, perhaps you have a natural fit for this type of responsibility, such as a user experience department. More likely, though, a number of departments or teams might be possible candidates for the job: web development, information technology, assessment, public services, reference or instruction services, systems, or digital initiatives. It may be a challenge to determine where in the organization the responsibility should reside. Since the website impacts nearly every department, and since organizational structures are often convoluted and responsibilities unclear, a library-wide discussion might be appropriate.

In smaller libraries, you may not have the luxury of selecting a department, since you have more generalists than specialists, and broader responsibilities given to a small number of library staff. In this case, thinking of individuals and their particular duties, interests, and skill sets is more realistic than thinking of the responsibilities of entire departments or teams.

Either way, wherever the responsibility lies within the organizational structure, it is best to put usability testing within an actual individual's job responsibilities. This accountability is key to sustaining usability testing over the long term. It doesn't need to be a significant piece of his or her daily work, but it ought to be documented in some manner as an expectation. At least a small percentage of that person's time should be dedicated to usability testing, whether it is written in a job description, reflected in annual goals, or managed through another internal process that your organization has established for this type of work. This ensures that there is a person responsible for securing resources for testing, planning for ongoing testing, and making sure improvements are made to the website based on the results of testing. This doesn't mean that one person will be responsible for actually conducting all usability testing. It just means that one person will be responsible for ensuring usability testing gets done, and gets done well.

The best person for this type of role is somebody who is service oriented, analytic, and passionate about improving the user experience. This person also needs to be excellent at organization and communication in order to coordinate testing across the library, manage the ongoing effort, and communicate the value of testing to stakeholders. Perhaps this person is you, or perhaps it is somebody who works close to you. Whatever the case, make usability testing part of somebody's ongoing job responsibilities, demonstrating that there is a commitment to it and ensuring that there is some level of organizational accountability.

Communicate Your Results

Library administrators must understand the importance of usability testing in order to support it, so you need to become an advocate. You need to continually make the case for usability testing in your organization, demonstrating the high return on investment. Usability testing requires both staff and financial resources, so its value must be communicated to those responsible for funding decisions. Fortunately, this isn't all that difficult.

Quantitative data can be very powerful. While you may not be conducting scientific research whereby data will actually prove or disprove something, you will gather data that indicates the extent of usability problems associated with particular tasks. Carefully track the success and failure rates of various tasks, as well as the number of attempts it takes to complete a given task. High failure rates on tasks, especially those very important to your organization, will be especially troubling for library administrators. Realizing that a significant portion of students cannot access e-books, or donors cannot sign up for an event, ought to raise concerns and give solid justification for putting resources into fixing the usability problems.

In chapter 7, you were introduced to a variety of methods for analyzing and representing data. Sharing results from testing can be particularly helpful to make your case to the library—to demonstrate why usability testing is so important. Use charts, graphs, or infographics to illustrate success rates, failure rates, and attempt rates. This can help illustrate the urgency of a particular usability problem, as well as illustrating where you are successful.

Qualitative data will be the bulk of your usability findings and can be just as powerful. Video is also a great way to engage your stakeholders in the process, so recording usability tests can be a useful habit to get into. Rather than playing entire tests, try to dedicate a little time to editing and pulling together video clips that are the most interesting or compelling. For instance, a montage of students struggling to sign into their library account, book a study room, or access a course guide can produce significant reactions from stakeholders who were not aware of the usability problems. Videos that demonstrate both the successes and failures of a website should be shared broadly with stakeholders. Celebrate the successes, and ask your library for a commitment to fix the failures.

Stories and quotes are also very convincing. Many of these could be captured in video, but even without a recording you may want to track quotes in your note taking that are especially worthy of sharing with others. For instance, a history student might remark, "I never knew you had online access to these images. This is amazing!" or might complain, "I don't understand why you force me to sign in just to see this image, which now won't even load on my computer." Again, both the positive and the negative comments should be captured and shared strategically among staff who would benefit from hearing them. Stories and quotes demonstrate value to your efforts in a way that it easy to digest and that can be engaging and meaningful to stakeholders.

Perhaps the most important thing to communicate is what decisions you made and what changes were implemented based on the results of usability testing, and how those changes have improved the user experience. Only the results of the changes truly demonstrate the value in usability testing. This can be a quantitative comparison of pretest and posttest success rates, analytics data that demonstrate higher usage of a particular page or section of the website, or videos of students expressing their appreciation for the website improvements.

While communicating with stakeholders should be an ongoing effort, you need to be careful not to overload them with information that will get lost in the shuffle. This is where having a communication strategy will help. For instance, you may want to send out monthly or quarterly e-mails to all library staff with highlights. You may want to organize presentations for all staff a couple of times a year. You could also host viewing parties where library staff gather together to watch and discuss usability testing results. A website or blog that you make available to the entire library might be a good option, where you can share detailed results, charts, videos, and progress made.

If you are working on a redesign project or making significant changes to your website, you may want to ramp up your communication efforts. This might include more frequent e-mails and presentations, more targeted presentations to particular groups, and more detailed analysis and presentation of data. No matter the frequency or mechanisms of your communication efforts, make sure you are using data to back up your decisions, demonstrating the impact of those decisions, and subsequently demonstrating the value of usability testing.

◎ Foster a User-Centered Culture

Focusing on the user experience is important, not just for those responsible for the library website, but for anyone who works on a service, resource, or product that involves interaction with users. Through enthusiastic and ongoing communication broadly across your library, you will begin to foster a culture that recognizes the importance of user experience.

Usability testing is something that everyone can learn how to do. Generate enthusiasm for improving the user experience, then provide information on how to conduct usability testing and conduct training sessions for those who are interested. Rather than having one usability expert on staff, you can have numerous staff members who have practiced and feel comfortable conducting usability tests on the fly.

Motivate library staff members to get involved and to share what they are doing within their own areas to improve the user experience. Give praise and recognition to those who make improvements, however small, based on user feedback.

Encourage people to think about the user experience at all opportunities. Begin to build some kind of variation on usability testing into every new service you offer, whether it is provided online or in person. Make it an assumption that the user experience will be tested before a new service is launched, or that there is a period of testing for the first few weeks after launch, in which feedback is actively gathered and adjustments are made.

Develop a training plan for library staff whose work impacts the user experience. In addition to giving them the tools to conduct their own usability testing, you can train them in such related topics as user experience design, form design, information architecture, writing for the web, content strategy, and do-it-yourself user research methods. Perhaps you can form a user experience interest group with library staff members from across the organization. You can provide trainings and workshops, watch webinars together, and share what you learn at conferences. You can also tackle usability problems as a group. By having each other as resources, you will motivate one another to continue to learn, and you will slowly but significantly grow the organizational knowledge and foster a user-centered culture.

◎ Commit to Continual Learning

As with almost any field, and especially with one related to technology, there is a constant growth in knowledge. You will continue to see new results from research studies, best practices and guides for success, and tools available to make your work easier. Because of this, it is essential that you commit time and energy to continual learning.

Stay up-to-date by paying attention to what is going on in the user experience field broadly, beyond the library community. Read articles and blogs, and subscribe to e-mail updates from those publishing content you find especially interesting. Online resources are a moving target, but some of the key websites for keeping up-to-date are currently

- Nielsen Norman Group: Evidence-Based User Experience Research, Training, and Consulting (http://www.nngroup.com)
- *Smashing Magazine* (http://www.smashingmagazine.com)
- User Interface Engineering (http://www.uie.com)
- *UX Magazine* (http://uxmag.com)

In addition to keeping yourself abreast of new developments in the field, it's important to build a network. Participate in groups on LinkedIn, such as User Experience and UX Professionals. Follow usability experts on Twitter, attend conferences, and participate in trainings and workshops. Reach out to other librarians focused on the user experience. Join e-mail lists to make connections with the library community, such as Web4Lib out of the University of Notre Dame and Usability4Lib out of the University of Rochester. Contribute to the conversation and share what you learn with others in the field by writing, presenting, and networking. Be proactive in building a user experience community within the library profession.

◎ Utilize Other User Research Methods

Usability testing is a method to test the usability of your website in a realistic fashion, but there are other user research methods that can also contribute to your decision making related to your website.

Surveys can be used to find out how users describe themselves and what they are expecting from or hoping to do on your website. This can be a useful tool for learning about your primary audience and their primary tasks, and can help you focus your attention on what matters the most to users.

User interviews and focus groups are a helpful tool for getting in-depth, subjective information from your users directly. This can be a great way to find out what your users' priorities are when it comes to your website. Interviews and groups can also be a way to learn about how users approach a problem, what language they use to describe things, and what improvements they would like to see on your website.

Card sorting is a method that allows you to find out how users think about labels, categories, and organization of content. Essentially, you place content on index cards and ask participants to sort them into categories. In an open card sort, the participant writes down labels for each category. In a closed card sort, the participant is given categories and is asked to place each content card underneath the given categories. A hybrid card sort may allow the participant to either use a given category or create his or her own.

Multivariate testing is a way to test what impact a single change can have on user behavior. This method is often conducted as an A/B test, in which there is version A and

OTHER USER RESEARCH METHODS

- Surveys
- User interviews
- Card sorting
- Multivariate testing

version B of your website, and is often used as a way to measure conversion rates if you are hoping for users to click on a particular thing. Users are presented with one of the two versions, and you then gather data on what the user clicks on, or doesn't click on.

As you build your knowledge of user experience, you will build your knowledge of user research methods. Beyond usability testing, you will want to incorporate these other types of methods at various times for various purposes. You may also want to build these methods into your ongoing efforts.

Key Points

Usability testing can be sustained over time with the right tools, people, and communication to keep up the momentum. Remember:

- Someone needs to be put in charge of usability testing and held accountable.
- Well-thought-out and purposeful communication is key for organizational buy-in.
- Aim toward a user-centered culture organization-wide.
- Never stop learning.
- Take advantage of other user research methods.

For a substantial cost, you can hire trained usability consultants who will conduct usability testing for your library in a professional and controlled manner. But with just a bit of practice and with an ongoing commitment, you can develop usability testing experts at your organization. Creating your own usability testing program is more practical and more sustainable, and will ultimately lead to remarkable improvements to the user experience.

Appendix: Example of a Usability Testing Report (Summary Version)

 Goals

To see if users can reserve a room or find information about study rooms at the main library. This is a revamped section of the website, so we wanted to test in the development site (webdev) before implementing these changes to the live website.

Testing Overview

We tested the revamped pages on a Windows laptop on four different days in September and October in the Main Library lobby, intercepting passersby to participate. We provided candy, snacks, and water to participants. Rachel was the facilitator and Monique was the note taker.

Nine people participated: eight undergraduate students, one graduate student. Not every participant was asked to complete every scenario.

Tasks and Scenarios

TASK	SCENARIO
Reserve a room for two people.	You need to find a room in the main library for yourself and a friend to work on a project. Find out if a study room is available and how to book it.
Find out if the library has rooms with computer technology.	You are working on a group project for class. Your group wants to get together and work on the PowerPoint presentation. Find out if the library has rooms that let you view the project on a big screen and where they are.

TASK	SCENARIO
Find a room for a large study group.	You have a group of friends who want to get together to study for an exam. Find the different options of where in the library you can meet together.

Findings

TASK	NUMBER OF PARTICIPANTS	NUMBER OF ATTEMPTS	SUCCESS RATE BY ATTEMPT	PERCENT SUCCESSFUL BY ATTEMPT	OVERALL SUCCESS RATE	OVERALL PERCENT SUCCESSFUL
Reserve a room for two people.	5	6	4/6	67%	4/5	80%
Find out if the library has rooms with computer technology.	4	7	3/7	43%	3/4	75%
Find a room for a large study group.	4	6	3/6	50%	3/4	75%

Big Themes and Patterns

- Most participants went directly to "Study Spaces and Computing," confirming that this label works well.
- Some participants had difficulty once they were on this page, but most were ultimately successful.
- Participants commented that the photos of the study rooms were helpful.

Useful Quotes

- "That's great that I can reserve a room. I didn't know that!"
- "It wasn't obvious to go to Services but after Services it was easy to find."
- "I probably would have searched first."
- "I would go to the information desk or use Ask a Librarian."

Different Audiences

Most participants followed similar paths and had similar problems. The two participants who were international students, whose English was a second language, struggled more to find the information.

⑥ Recommendations

USABILITY PROBLEM	RECOMMENDATIONS
Participants went to the correct web page, but couldn't find out how to get a specific type of study room.	Reorganize the content on this web page to organize study rooms by two features (e.g., technology, quiet) and by number of people.
Participants went to "University Libraries" and "Main Library" but didn't see anything about study rooms.	Add more content to the "Main Library" web page, including information about study rooms.

⑥ Other Themes

THEME	WHAT THIS MEANS
Participants were not aware that you could reserve study rooms.	We should better promote this new service both on the website and in person (perhaps signs on the doors of the study rooms themselves).
Participants mentioned going to the campus website to look for information on study spaces.	We should look at the campus website and make sure students can find out about library study rooms if they start there, rather than look on our website directly.

Index

large-scale testing. *See* controlled testing
length of tests, 13, 54, 67–68. *See also* time
life cycle of usability testing, 102
location, 54–56. *See also* setup

mobile devices. *See* hardware
moderated remote testing. *See* remote testing
moderation. *See* facilitation
multivariate testing. *See* other user research methods

navigation: capturing, 76–78; elements, 31, 98, 108,
    110–111; labels, 97; paths, 97
Nielsen, Jakob, 3, 13
Nielsen Norman Group, x, 13, 123
note taking, 43–44, 75–80; example, 80; template, 78

observation room. *See* observing
observer effect. *See* Hawthorne Effect
observing, 11, 57, 76. *See also* software
ongoing testing, 6, 12–13, 29–30
other user research methods, 4, 8, 19, 21, 123–24

paper prototypes, 98, 108, 110
participants: number of, 13; role of, 3. *See also* audience
personas, 25–26
primary audience. *See* audience
primary tasks. *See* tasks
problems, usability, 9–10; prioritizing, 92–93; root cause
    of, 94
processes. *See* workflows

retesting, 101–102
recording, 11, 12, 57. *See also* software
recruitment, 57–62; defining audience for, 30–33; formal,
    36–37; inclusion and exclusion criteria, 59–61;
    intercept, 36, 57–60; targeted, 33–34, 59–61
redesign, 13, 20, 30, 108–111, 117
Redish, Ginny, 98
release forms, 57, 66
remote testing, 40–42
report, written 102–103, 125–127
retrospective review, 72, 83
role: of facilitator, 3, 9, 70–75; of note taker, 75–80; of
    participant, 3
Rubin, Jeffrey, 68, 72, 92, 94
rules, for participants, 68–69

scenarios: ordering, 51–53; translating from tasks,
    48, 52; writing, 48–51. *See also* tasks
schedule, testing on a, 113–14
screen capture. *See* recording; software
screen sharing. *See* observing
screening questions, 59–61, 66–67. *See also* recruitment
search, testing, 45
secondary audience. *See* audience
setup, 57–58, 62
software, 11, *12*, 41–42, 57. *See also* technology
solutions to usability problems: brainstorming, 9,
    86; identifying, 95–97; implementing, 98–100,
    104
source of error analysis, 94
staffing, 12, 101, 104, 113
stakeholders, 86–87, 103, 120–22
statistical significance, 92. *See also* Institutional Review
    Board (IRB)
subjects. *See* participants
success and failure to complete tasks: analyzing,
    89–92; compiling, 87; documenting, 77; identifying,
    80–82; measuring again after a change, 101–102;
    removing tasks based on, 48; sharing, 121. *See also*
    tasks
suggestions from participants, 74
surveys, 19, 21. *See also* other user research methods
systematic testing. *See* ongoing testing

talk-aloud. *See* think-aloud
tasks: attempts to complete, 77, 89; defining primary
    16–22, *24*–25; defining successful completion, 46–47;
    number of, 48; selecting which to test,
    44–46; translating into scenarios, 48, 52; writing,
    46–48. *See also* scenarios; success and failure to
    complete tasks
team testing, 75
technical knowledge. *See* audience, different behavior or
    knowledge
technology, 10–12, 41–42, 56–57; local vs. participant,
    39–40
test subjects. *See* participants
testing: in the field, 38; in the lab, 37–38
think-aloud, 71–72
time: commitment, 12–13; introducing for testing,
    67–68; running out of, 81–83; selecting for testing,
    53–54. *See also* length of tests

time on task, 71, 87, 91

tools. *See* software

trigger words, 50–52, 79–80, 90

unmoderated remote testing. *See* remote testing

usability professionals, 4, 30. *See also* controlled testing

usability testing, definition of, 3

user interviews. *See* other user research methods

user journeys, 5, 26–27, 69, 93

web analytics, 21, 56

workflows, 34, 111–114, 116

About the Author

Rebecca Blakiston has been a librarian at the University of Arizona Libraries since 2008, and the website product manager since 2010. She provides oversight, management, and strategic planning for the library website, specializing in guerilla usability testing, writing for the web, and content strategy. She chairs a website steering group and meets regularly with staff from across the library to facilitate communication, training, and collaboration. She developed a process for in-house usability testing, which has been implemented successfully both within website projects and in an ongoing, systematic way.

In 2012, Rebecca was project manager for the complete rebuild and redesigns of two archive and research center websites at the University of Arizona: Special Collections and the Center for Creative Photography. In 2014, she was project manager for another ambitious project: the complete rebuild and redesign of the main website for the University of Arizona Libraries. She led the user research efforts for all of these projects, which included surveys, focus groups, card sorting, and, of course, usability testing.

In 2013, Rebecca organized the six-course certificate program in user experience for Library Juice Academy, and she teaches the online courses Do-It-Yourself Usability Testing, Writing for the Web, and Developing a Website Content Strategy. She has presented extensively on usability testing and other user research methods, website content strategy, and website redesign efforts. She advocates for ongoing, systematic efforts to improve the user experience, and she hopes that you do the same.